THE WAR NEXT DOOR

MY JOURNEYS INTO UKRAINE

WILL BLACKBURN never meant to write a book about Ukraine. For many years he was happy selling software and living in London. The only outstanding drama in his life had been a tour of Iraq with the Territorial Army in 2003/4.

A family crisis in 2015 precipitated a move to Poland. In February of 2022 Will and his wife found themselves living right on the border of a massive European war. He knew he could not stand by and be happy selling software. It was time to do something.

Once Will saw for himself the utter destruction and suffering of Ukraine and its people, he realised that he had to document what he was seeing. Those notes became the book that he never meant to write about Ukraine, *The War Next Door*.

Will is now fully involved in sourcing equipment in support of Ukraine and the convoys run by Fundacja Igora Tracza.

THE WAR NEXT DOOR

MY JOURNEYS INTO UKRAINE

Will Blackburn

Marble Hill London

First published by Marble Hill Publishers in 2024

Flat 58 Macready House
75 Crawford Street
London W1H 5LP
www.marblehillpublishers.co.uk

A CIP catalogue record for this book is available from the
British Library.

ISBN: 9781738497003
E-book ISBN: 9781738497034

Text and jacket design by Paul Harpin
Cover image © Maryna Kriuchenko | Dreamstime.com
Printed and bound by IngramSpark

DEDICATIONS

This book is dedicated to:

My darling wife Jula, your support and love have sustained me both in Ukraine and the writing of this book. None of this could have happened without you, my love.

The late great Babcia Ola – whose inspiring courage and fortitude symbolised all that is wonderful about Poland.

Mummy and Daddy for all your loving support and for proving that hard manual labour is an option for octogenarians seeking work.

George, Caleb, Joshua and Martha – for all your love, encouragement and guidance.

John Eminson – it took me thirty-five years to get there but your advice about finding my voice stayed with me throughout the writing of this book. God bless you, John.

Phil Dodd – for encouraging me in 1995 to write something. I'm just a slow starter Phil!

THANKS

Thank you, Rover Group Iraq 2003/4, – Kiwi, Dave, Billy, Mark, Tommy, Richard, Skippy, Matt, Paul, Scott, Chris, Neil and Pete – the skills you taught me all those years ago have been invaluable. I think of you often when I am in Ukraine.

Everyone who so generously donated much needed equipment for Ukraine. Special mention must be made of Jason Gwynne, Paula Massey and the community of www.arrse.co.uk

Rob Baker – without you and your support the whole donations process simply would not have worked. I cannot thank you enough.

To all the incredibly brave Poles and Ukrainians of Fundacja Igora Tracza who I have had the great privilege of travelling to Ukraine with; Igor, Jacek, Michel, Krystian, Anatoliy, Maciek, Sacha, Ira, Aga, Mania, all of you – your bravery and dedication are extraordinary. You truly go and continue to go where angels fear to tread. My heart is full of the most profound love and respect for you all.

David Peake – for promoting our cause online and co-ordinating donations.

To all of you, thank you.

AUTHOR'S NOTE

For obvious reasons I have changed the names of some of my Ukrainian friends mentioned in the book. Perhaps one day when this cruel war is over, their real names can be revealed. For now, and for their own safety, place names and the names of some individuals must remain a secret.

TABLE OF CONTENTS

Chapter 1

PUTIN INVADES!

I AM AWAKE. The room is bathed in a cold ethereal light, the afterglow of an update. That algorithmic media alarm which always beats my old analogue clock by about twelve minutes, never leaving quite enough time for a snooze. Easier to check the update and embrace the day, just as the algorithm intends.

Normal mornings reveal a list of click bait that can be ignored, allowing an effortless move from breakfast into comforting routine. Then there are those rare days when the adrenaline wash of the unbelievable throws priority and routine into free-fall.

"They are moving into Ukraine, Jula, it's happening."

I was fumbling for the TV control and the BBC news. The sassy presenter was already halfway through the latest bulletin. A deluge of information. Rooftop reportage. Panic. Morphing graphics outlining Ukraine. I noted our current location, a greyed-out bay just in the top left corner. Kaliningrad a sobering Dover to Calais distance from that same blank bay that we called home.

What to do? We telephoned our Ukrainian tenants, Ivanka and Zbigniew, in London. Were they OK?

"Are YOU OK?" came right back at us, "You guys are closer than we are."

The sudden reality of Poland's long border with Ukraine and three-hundred-kilometer border with Russia was being reinforced in real time by the arrows and images on various screens. Hastily suited pundits from the relevant faculties and institutions were being wheeled in to predict the worst, or confirm the range of some lumbering on-screen mechanical monster tanking along an innocent highway.

"My brother is getting his wife and kids together and they are heading for the Slovakian border," a Facetime Ivanka reported over a long-forgotten bowl of cereal. Her normally happy voice dampened into an everything-has-changed-for-ever tone. I remember meeting her brother's kids on a trip to London. Impossibly well behaved, impossibly cute. To think of them being hastily stuffed into a neighbour's van and racing to an uncertain border was bewildering. The very little one's peeping face came to mind, sat on our sofa in London only a few years before. I remembered her encyclopaedic knowledge of cartoons. By now she was racing down country lanes and barely used forest roads in a bid to outrun the Russian monster.

"Your father predicted this, Ivanka," said Jula.

Indeed, he had. I recalled an evening shortly after 2014 when Russia invaded Crimea and the Donbas. My woeful DIY attempts were being rectified by the kindly hands of Vasil, Ivanka's father. I was holding up a shower rail (while he remeasured my hopeless efforts) when he quietly announced that Russia would expand the war as soon as Moscow was ready. I agreed, making some second-rate comment about the Sudetenland and appeasement. Jula and Vasil then descended into the shared Slavic experiences of Russian aggression, repression and fear, a common bond that unites all those countries that sadly share a border with Russia.

"What are YOU going to do Jula?" came Ivanka's

response. The news was already showing blocked roads and refugees heading for the Polish border.

"We will stay and fight," said Jula in a voice I had never heard in all our married life. It visibly shocked Ivanka. It shocked me. There was no irony, or dark humour in her statement. Only a sad Polish acceptance, a reflex action, born of never really having had a choice but to fight. Everything had changed in an hour. A 9/11 feeling in the guts.

The call ended shortly afterwards as Ivanka wanted an update on family progress.

Jula turned to me and said in the September tones of Chamberlain. "We have a war next door now, William. A war next door."

Chapter 2

EARLY DAYS

A DAY AFTER the invasion I was walking through our local park. The benches and lawns seemed strangely and aimlessly busy. There was a sense of people gathering without purpose. Lost with no intention of being lost. Women were crying into mobile phones, clinging onto overfilled prams. Older men were gathered in groups exchanging scraps of paper and nodding with a stern insular concentration. At first, I did not make the connection, what on earth was going on? The normal rhythm and vibe of the park was usually very laid back. Yet on this day there was a palpable anxiety, a listlessness that rendered the park as incongruous and unfamiliar as the gathering people. It was as though someone had superimposed a botanical garden where a busy bus station should be.

Refugees!! Of course! In that moment of sudden realisation I caught the red watery eyes of a young woman seated on a bench. She gave me a sad smile and then returned to waving at a young man in uniform on screen. A child sat on her lap giggling and twisting. The magnitude of the last twenty-four hours lost in childish adventure and very little sleep.

"Why didn't you come with us Daddy?" asked the child.

I moved on. The three-dimensional grief of actual refugees suddenly overwhelming and shocking.

Like a coward I hurried home. These were people who

truly needed help, yet somehow when confronted with the physical reality of Ukrainian refugees I did not know what to do. Sympathy for people on a TV is easy to manage, real suffering harder to comprehend. Should I stop and comfort them? Was that crossing a boundary? These were homeless people who were not homeless people. Regular homeless people understand the hurrying past, the lack of eye contact. It is part of the gig. Refugees though, they fix you with haunting eyes, needy, helpless and displaying none of the street smarts that permit you to wander past traditional homeless people, guilt free. The refugee gaze is more spiritually loaded. Emotionally complex. A telepathic cry for help, dignity and disaster in equal measure. A primeval look that you could only display to fellow humans if your home was on fire and everything you had known had been destroyed only twelve hours before. A look that cannot be faked. The refugee also carries an aura of fear that says, "You are next."

Approaching home, I saw an unnatural queue was forming down our street. The tiny one-in one-out passport photo shop was doing its best to accommodate a nervous mixture of mothers, children and bewildered elderly Ukrainians. A Puffa jacketed lady, all muffler and smartphone intertwined, relayed directions back to someone clearly needing fast, compliant photos.

"No Oksana, I'm in the queue. Just get yourself here and we can work something out."

Walking along that desperate line I felt as though a parallel universe had materialised. The people in the queue, gaunt, adrenaline- driven, were functioning on another level of stunned consciousness. Some were dressed immaculately, others in hastily covered pyjamas, whatever was at hand when the orders came to run. I tried to say good morning to one or two people but they were completely lost in their own anxious bubbles of empty purses, terror and half eaten donated biscuits. The elderly stood resigned in stark contrast to the young mothers yelling at their children as a release. Different ways of masking the pain and coming to terms with the absolute free-fall of their instantly destroyed lives.

A message beeped on my phone. It was the owner of our favourite beach bar. "Please come over and talk when you can."

It was as easy to divert to the beach as to go home. I found Mikolai at the bar. He launched straight into conversation.

"Do we fight? Do we go and fight?" There was no agitation just anger. We had talked many times before about Polish history and the dangers of Putin's Russia. As if to add another level of hyper-reality to the situation, if I squinted my eyes through the beach-facing window behind Mikolai I could just about make out a distant light speck. Kaliningrad. Fighting was not idle talk. The enemy were only a 30 km boat ride away.

Just then, Mikolai's Ukrainian chef came barreling out of the kitchen brandishing her phone. On screen her bear of an uncle was waving a hunting rifle and running with friends in the snow. They yelled and whooped with a weird, nothing matters anymore euphoria, gathering around some form of Russian vehicle. Proud and angry tears bubbled from the chef's helpless face. Mikolai calmed her down and told her that this Englishmen (meaning me) had been in the British Army and would help get them equipment. The chef suddenly cheered up and shook my hand as though the fate of Ukraine rested solely with me!!

Mikolai sat me down and then very worryingly gave me a free coffee.

"They need boots," he said. "Socks, helmets and food. Can you help?"

I thought of all the peaceful summer evenings we had spent in those same seats. Balmy, happy times. Now, on that bleak February day I was hunched over our usual table, talking in hushed tones and nodding conspiratorially. Normal life was ebbing away from our quiet town. Downing the coffee, I stood up. "I will see what I can do." It all felt very "Secret Army" 2.0.

On the way back to our apartment I thought about the chef's uncle, the mad panic in the snow. The faces of the refugees. How could we help?

I spoke with Jula about fighting and what it would mean. The uncertainty. The chances of survival. Massive life questions which seemed so far removed from the simple existence we were enjoying only 24 hours before. We would oscillate between deep fear and stomping anger as image after image confirmed Russia's medieval treatment of defenceless people.

I thought of when we first met. Our life had been so unconsciously safe in leafy London. For many years our greatest fears had been the big mortgage and losing our jobs. We were now 30 km from a border with Russia, a Russia that was smashing its way into another neighbouring country. A friend from Spain called telling us to pack a bag and run.

"At least make a plan," he said as I told him we were staying and would fight. "Really Will, REALLY? You are a middle-aged man. Think about it!"

I was thinking about it. It was all I was thinking about! I had served in the TA and am an Iraq veteran. It was a chapter in my life that I had eventually packed away. It sat like a rusty locked box in my mental attic, a box that on some days I chose to open and pour over. Maybe too much sometimes. Now speaking with Jula about the madness unfolding on our screens, half remembered fears and knowledge came back to me. The smells, the weight of kit, the fear, a strange mix of what can bother you from a twenty-year-old memory. I also found myself feeling nostalgic for Iraq. For that illogical, controllable quality of the past. The kindly software of memory, falsely creating a better version of the what, when and how.

The luxury of Iraq was its abstraction. The danger was seemingly contained in the Middle East. It was possible to leave that danger behind by virtue of distance. However bad things became over there, a massive fire break existed between those two worlds. Basra could be hell but the knowledge of being able to return to quiet suburban streets was comforting in its safety and consistency. The war tap could be turned off if your home was the UK.

Sitting in our Polish home there was no such fire break. We had a war next door. Refugees were already a very visible presence in the streets and parks. Our town was less than a one-day drive from smouldering tanks and bodies in the street. Poland knew only too well from history what a marauding Russian Army meant. Poles also knew that nothing had changed. They knew this long before the murders began in Bucha and Irpin. As with much of Eastern Europe, Poland's folk memories are shaped and structured by the constant crushing Russian evil that has stalked their land for a millennium. Russia always acting as the apex geopolitical predator. The West does not really understand the reflex fear left by such constant aggression, best illustrated by the allies's lack of desire to address the trail of horror left by Moscow post the victory of '45. The truth about the Soviet Union was carefully hidden by the uncomfortable shuffling of the "fellow travellers" in the west and those organisations who carefully managed the inconvenient truths surrounding Soviet victory. The effects of that Russian murder train lived long in the memories of those who survived.

I saw that terrible legacy of damage firsthand one haunting night, manifested in the blank eyes of my wife's Granny (Babcia). When Babcia became too frail to care for herself we moved back to Poland to ensure her last years were comfortable and protected. She was a joy to be around, and I was fascinated by Babcia's story. She had survived the Nazis and Communism. She had run through fields of total war and witnessed destruction beyond comprehension. And yet she was a bundle of fun and love, seemingly undamaged by her early life. For many years Babcia and I had danced around the subject of the war. She always politely smiled and said we must focus on the present.

A lifetime of living under totalitarian government had given her a survivor's ability to deflect questions with a delicate, closing grace. Years of media training could never achieve Babcia's mercurial conversational skill. Question the question until the subject ceased to exist or the moment passed. This obfuscation only fuelled my desire to discover Granny's story in the naïve belief that some imagined catharsis would result from the telling. In my arrogance I thought that aged 93 it was important that she told us her story, and that somehow this knowledge could be woven into the fabric of the family story. Happy-ever-after closure would surely be guaranteed?

I can see her now, illuminated in the chiaroscuro of her reading lamp. The comforting, well-loved handmade cardigan. Her favourite chocolates arranged neatly on a plate. The perfect picture of a cuddly, lovely, smiley Granny. She seemed so relaxed and happy. Jula was out with friends. In regrettable ignorance I thought that settled evening would be the right moment to ambush her with my war questions. She ambushed me right back with her answers.

Following the sudden unsolicited gear shift of my opening question: "How did you get here from the East, Granny? You must have walked though terrible fighting."

The cogs began whirring and Granny flicked her hands in a nervous convulsion. Something told me right away that I had broken the seal on a vial of bad memories with more bad energy than I could handle. A tension was building. I felt like the Sorcerer's apprentice, completely unprepared for what she had to say and completely unqualified to handle the carefully controlled trauma that I had unleashed. Out came the horror in convulsive chunks of information. The systematic rape. The cruel murder. The locust-like theft of everything and anything, regardless of value. A Russian Army on the rampage. The words came in an almost supernatural stream of consciousness. Her voice completely changed in the telling. It was a hard voice, a long forgotten, smothered, stifled primal scream of a voice.

I will never forget her eyes. The sparkly love of her blue eyes had completely disappeared. In recalling those buried nightmares, the life had gone, replaced by an ocular abyss. There was nothing to maintain contact with just dead, hopeless eyes.

I was truly terrified. The unholy darkness in her stare was demonstrative of a waking nightmare. I was truly out of my depth. Granny gradually began to calm herself, slowly leaving the forbidden zone her mind had dropped into. The incident maybe lasted only ten minutes but it left poor Granny exhausted and deeply distressed. Finally, as if to break the spell, she asked for some vanilla ice cream which I rushed to grab from the kitchen. Anything to assuage the crushing guilt of what I had done. She wolfed down the ice cream and self-medicating on fat and sugar her eyes slowly returned to normal. The relief. I gave her a massive hug and she hugged me back whilst giving me a be-careful-what-you-wish-for glance. By bedtime I thought Granny had recovered. Wrong again. That night I heard her feeble, childish voice calling out in vain for her Mummy and Daddy. I felt utterly ashamed of what I had done and still do.

The darkness and pain I witnessed that night we all

wrongly believed was consigned to the past. We all thought that somehow Russia had moved on from that Stalinist brutality hidden by the 1945 victory and subsequent Cold War. This was in fact a post-Soviet con trick perpetrated by Putin. The Russians are just as wicked as they have ever been.

News from Bucha and Irpin confirmed all our worst fears. Russia displaying the same murderous behaviour that dear Granny had endured eighty years before. It was time to think about how we could really help Ukraine. We reached the conclusion that Kyiv did not need a middle-aged man with out-of-date military skills. My anger and ego were not going to make a ha'porth of difference to the outcome. It was time to come up with a different plan.

Chapter 3.
THIS IS WHAT THEY NEED

OVER THE NEXT few days we bought and donated dry food, nappies, even Babcia's favourite woolly coat. We donated that directly to a wonderfully brave Ukrainian lady. She had just brought her children out of Ukraine. Now they were safe with relatives she was going to drive a van full of supplies back to her hometown and bring back more refugees.

"What are you going to do after that?" I asked.

"I come back and open hair shop in Poland," she replied, as if this was the most normal thing in the world. She did exactly that too. Incredible.

The volunteers at the local depot were helping the refugees arriving in the town while simultaneously co–ordinating deliveries of aid to Ukraine. The food and supplies seemed only to come from the UK or Poland. That surprised me, bearing in mind the geography - more than a few wealthy EU countries stood between the UK and Poland.

"Great Britain always helps," said one of the aid volunteers.

We were only a week into the war. Already individuals and local groups from the UK had bandied together, collected food and essentials and delivered them to Poland. I felt very proud and humbled at the same time. The soft power of such UK support was not lost on the Poles or Ukrainians either.

THIS IS WHAT THEY NEED

"I've been told what you really need is boots, helmets, socks and med kit," I said.

The volunteer stopped and looked up. It was as though I had repeated a magic password. A code that opened another door.

"You can get these things!? You know where to get them!? These are the most important things."

Instant VIP status. The volunteer was immediately joined by a supervisor. My wife helped translate when we all got a bit too enthusiastic or stuck on a word. We left the depot with everyone shaking my hand as though I was the 21st century's answer to the Marshall plan.

"What did you tell them?" I asked Jula.

"I said you had lots of Army kit at home," she replied, in the way that wives do in casual disregard of their better halves' possessions.

She was right. During my time in the Territorial Army I had accumulated all manner of kit and gadgets. The military hoarding had reached alarming proportions just prior to being mobilised and sent to Iraq. The result was a veritable baggage train of boxes and buckshee kit that had followed me round for the last two decades. It had even followed me to Poland.

Jula had often asked me why I hung onto all this stuff? There was no practical or logical reason for doing so. I have a feeling my military hoarding served a psychological Dorian Grey-like purpose. For as long as your kit is in the attic – you are still vital. Still young and needed, a slumbering Arthurian knight, waiting until called upon to save a kingdom in peril. Yes! That hidden helmet and webbing were simply waiting for a quixotic adventure to justify their storage. In a weird sort of way, I had been half right in hanging onto them.

Once home, I did indeed find my helmet and webbing stuffed in a box in Babcia's old room. The helmet still fitted, the padded lining felt cold, compressing the aroma of the past over my face. The smells reminded me of Iraq. Thoughts of quixotic adventure rapidly dissipated into the realities of what I had seen wearing that same dome all those years before. I was lost in my thoughts when Jula appeared with a pile of desert combat fatigues. Dumping them on the floor she disappeared as suddenly as she had arrived.

"I know where there is more," she called, her voice trailing off as though the more of my kit she donated the better off we would all be. Once again, I noted that in the democratic world of marriage similar luxuries are very rarely extended to better halves!

By early evening we had quite a respectable pile of kit, combat trousers x4, combat shirts x4, a military rucksack, boots, webbing and helmet. Almost enough to equip a whole soldier! I found something else too – a first field dressing. In civilian parlance a battlefield bandage that soaks up massive amounts of blood. I looked at the packaging and remembered being issued two before deploying to Iraq. One I wore on my body armour. The other....wait a minute....I used to keep in the top pocket of my Bergen rucksack.....I began feeling in the top pocket and there it was hidden away. Still box fresh after twenty years!

I thought of all the thousands of FFDs that must have been issued to soldiers over the years. Then I had another thought. If I still have my two issued FFDs – how many other veterans do? I photographed the bandage and stuck the picture on social media encouraging veterans to contact me if they still had one at home, and if they did could they send it to me?

Having posted my message, we then headed back up to the depot to deliver my old army kit. No sooner were we through the door than we were met by the organisers who spirited us into a side room as though protecting us from prying eyes. There they marvelled over the camouflage clothing and equipment. One of the inspecting volunteers looked up both moved and impressed that we had kept our word.

"These will go straight to the battalion we are supporting. Igor will be so very pleased".

That was the first time I had heard Igor's name mentioned. It would not be the last.

"Please, we need more equipment, socks, boots anything for soldiers, help soldiers, civilians OK now, we need fighting clothes and shoes."

"Fighting clothes and shoes". The words sounded so innocent, almost funny. The horrible truth was that Ukraine was desperately trying to field and equip an army. This volunteer had just come back from Ukraine and had seen young men and women heading into winter battles wearing gym kit and trainers.

"Please, anything," she said, holding up my old combats as though they were sacred relics.

We left the side room and found the corridor filling with a Ukrainian family that needed a starter pack of food and some shoes for the children. The mother greeted us very warmly and conversed with us while we were all offered tea and biscuits. I noticed my phone had been beeping quite a bit. I hid around a corner so not to seem rude and was surprised to see a dozen or so messages from a Fred in Carlisle, a Dave in Cardiff. They nearly all began with words to the effect of, "You don't know me but......."

Reading through the messages, it was clear that my hunch about veterans hoarding bandages was correct! The immediate concern now was where they should send them. I took a risk and provided them with our old London address. I would sort out the logistics with Ivanka, our Ukrainian tenant, later!

Heading back round the corner, I showed the

messages to my wife and the volunteer. Again, she herded us both back into that side room. I was starting to see that a careless talk costs lives mindset was beginning to be adopted. In time of war not everyone is your friend. We were also moving through the looking glass of involvement. Turn up with a bag of flour and it is a case of, "Please leave it there, thank you so much for your support." Turn up with military kit and you are now expressing a level of involvement which becomes a trust-building exercise.

"You know these people?"

"Well, they are veterans, I can see online that they have served in the army."

"OK, good. Let's see if they send."

There was a positive cynicism in the volunteer's voice. Almost, I do not doubt you, but the internet will let you down feel to her "Let's see if they send" remark.

We shook hands and promised to stay in regular contact. I told Jula of my plan to use our London apartment as a depot. Jula gave me that not-another-back-of-a -fag-packet-plan look that she has come to perfect over the years.

I phoned Ivanka. As a Ukrainian holding down a job in London and not able to provide much support for her home nation, she was thrilled to be helping. She forgave my fait accompli (probably breaching umpteen clauses in our tenancy agreement!) and promised to handle the deliveries.

The plan was that I would collect the little parcels on my regular visits to the UK and return to Poland with them in my hand luggage. Ivanka phoned me about a week later. She switched on her phone camera. Scanning the flat the scene was pure "Blue Peter" post bag. Lumpy parcels from Wrexham, packets from Leeds. An engineering firm had sent a 25kg box of all manner of medical trauma kit.

"Pleeeeez Vill, Pleeeesz, I not opens front door. It's

leeettle bit crazy now," said a bewildered Ivanka.

"All for Ukraines," came Ivanka's commentary as the camera panned around her parcel stuffed living room. I was simultaneously moved and concerned by the diminishing space of her little London flat cum warehouse.

A few days later I was in London. Hand luggage was out of the question. I purchased one of those ridiculously large suitcases that are effectively a wardrobe on wheels. We managed to cram 40 kgs worth of medical supplies in the case and another 15kgs in my hand luggage! The trip to the airport was a pure slapstick adventure of bumping stairs and balancing escalators. I only managed the journey due to the kindness of strangers, random people grabbing handles and steadying me on platforms, or half-pushing me into carriages.

At the airport, even before I had checked the wheeled monster into the hold, Ivanka was on the phone again. More parcels had arrived! I looked at the attendant checking me in. She was stifling a giggle as I struggled to lug the case onto the scales. All I could think of was poor Ivanka surrounded by packages again. My expensive and poorly executed logistics plan was clearly not sustainable. What to do?

As I was sitting in the pure luxury of Luton Airport's airside waiting area, I had another brainwave. Gzegorz. Maybe Gzegorz could help?

Moving to Poland eight years previously, we had used a wonderful company called Kamyktrans run by a very jolly and industrious Polish gentleman named Gzegorz. Nothing was too much trouble for him and his crew. I remember the team navigating impossible angles and stairs to remove sofas, exercise bikes, all the usual detritus of a house move. Everything was delivered to Poland intact and in record time. I dug out the number on my phone. Within minutes Gzegorz had agreed to collect and deliver the donations.

Ivanka could now relax in the knowledge that at least she would only be denied access to her apartment for a limited amount of time - or at least until Gzegorz made another collection.

This process worked beautifully until Ivanka bought herself a house up North. She assured me that it had nothing to do with the South London Parcel Room that her flat had become! The new tenants were not really onboard with becoming an aid depot, so the operation was switched to my parents' house. Big garage, and very lovely parents.

As with Ivanka, my elderly Mum and Dad suddenly found themselves shifting parcels every day. By the time I arrived to help with the first Gzegorz collection, dear Ma and Pa were on first name terms with all the Parcel Force, DHL and UPS drivers within about a 50-mile radius. Their garage (which disturbingly was about 5 square metres bigger than our London flat) was so full that the car had to stay on the drive. More importantly, shifting 10kg parcels all day is not necessarily a healthy pastime for octogenarians. What they had achieved was impressive, but as I watched them shuffling around the garage, I realised I had inadvertently created some form of old folks gulag. Dad's pride had him piling up very heavy boxes that anyone would struggle to lift. He just wanted to be doing his bit, bless him! A new plan would have to be made.

A solution presented itself at the Remembrance Sunday lunch in the next-door village of Chedworth. There, members of the local British Legion very graciously gave me the floor to talk about what we were trying to achieve in support of Ukraine. Immediately veterans young and old began to pipe up, offering boots, jackets, helmets. Both very moving and further confirmation of my military hoarding theory!

Two men in particular stepped forward, David and

Robert. David offered to spread the word throughout the local community and co– ordinate the collection of clothing and donations. Robert crucially offered to act as the new depot for parcels and boxes. I was relieved as this would mean my parents could retire from their second warehousing career.

Jason Gwynne from my old school, Cheltenham College, became an excellent supporter and provider of all manner of kit and donations.

On the medical side military veteran Paula Massey was the go-to person and all-round good egg when it came to sourcing and providing donations of medical kit. Her persistence delivered specialist bandages, crutches, breathing apparatus and all manner of paramedical equipment. There are many people alive today because of her important and timely contributions.

In terms of donations the biggest and most comprehensive source of military kit came from www.arrse.co.uk

I had been a member of the Army Rumour Service (ARRSE) site for years and had come to know and love the characters, the banter and the occasional campaigning. In 2007 ARRSE had been an important catalyst in galvanising veteran support for the purchase of accommodation for veterans' families, while their wounded loved ones recovered at Headley Court. An early doors example of the positive power of social media and the internet.

Through ARRSE I made a simple request for kit for Ukraine and was inundated with offers of all manner of boots, clothing and ancillary equipment for life in the field. With our new "warehouse", a constant stream of donations and a transport system in place we were all set to supply Ukraine with what they really needed.

Chapter 4
HOW I MET IGOR

THE KIT WE were bringing into Poland was in very high demand. Haemostatic bandages, boots, helmets and tourniquets were badly needed by the Ukrainian army. The networks in Poland were already beginning to settle into those who drove supplies to the main hubs in Ukraine and those who drove desperately needed kit right to the front line itself.

One name kept cropping up in conversation, mentioned in hushed tones. With nods and boasts, "my best friend's brother went to school with him," was enough to win admiring looks. "I have met him," another would say, their street cred lifted to a higher plain.

I had of course heard the name before. Igor. He had driven my original donation of kit to a battalion in Ukraine.

Gzegorz's December delivery to our Polish home (at almost a tonne) was the biggest so far. We immediately found ourselves living in a sea of boxes. A photo was sent to Ivanka who seemed delighted at our predicament. We needed Igor to come and collect direct.

Obtaining Igor's contact details was pure Ian Fleming, a labyrinthine process of confirming identities, commitment and clandestine conversations. So much so that when I finally reached the great man, I felt more than a little nervous.

"Hello Igor? My name is Will and I have been collecting equip...."

"Yes, I know who you are."

The words were said in that ambiguous, part sinister, part impatient way that busy people adopt in the unforgiving minute. The Polish accent enhanced the slightly menacing edge of the response.

"Give me your address and I will find you."

A hundred Cold War movies came to mind. I trotted out the address in full obedience. Transport was promised within the hour.

Jula and I waited nervously. When the doorbell rang we rushed around like frightened rabbits, grabbing the wrong coats, unable to find footwear right in front of us, nervous energy making us forget the simplest of actions.

"Where are the keys?"

"Keys?"

"Yes, keys to open the door!"

Fumbling with the lock we almost tumbled out of the door only to be greeting by the beaming face of Igor, with his lovely wife, Aga! In an instant my fear dissipated. One of Igor's team was already backing a transit van into our car park.

After some quick introductions I ran Igor through all the donated equipment. It was quite a list, and some kit was very specific. The brand-new chain saw for example! For a moment he stopped as if vexed by an invisible dilemma. He was facing away from me staring at a pile of boxes. I was starting to get the fear again. Had we got this wrong?

Igor turned his head and fixed me with a warm smile. "This is excellent. Very good, VERY GOOD!"

He was already checking the quality of the helmets and nodding. He looked at me again as if to say, "You are the real deal." It felt like I had passed a test.

Moving the equipment into the transit van, the neighbour's curtains began twitching. There was a moment where all five of us trooped out in single file, each carrying the exact same model of helmet and rucksack. Stacking my helmet and Bergen into the van I caught the eye of a neighbour who looked at me as if to say, "I won't tell." It all felt very 'Ryan's daughter.' Here we were supplying the great Igor with military kit!

Van fully loaded, we asked Igor if they wanted to stay for tea, as you do after loading a tonne of military kit destined for a war zone. Back in our apartment it was lovely to have our box-free corridors and rooms once more. I felt a belated solidarity with Ivanka.

Now more relaxed after all the lifting and shifting Igor and Aga explained how they balanced Ukraine aid deliveries with the challenges of dog-sledding. Yes, I should have mentioned that Igor is also a World Champion dog-sledder and all-round Alpha male!

"How can we help you more?" I asked as Igor explained the big pre-Christmas convoy he was planning.

"Do you want to come with us?"

The question was delivered in the most matter-of-fact way. Completely devoid of drama. It was as though we were talking about taking a lift to the shops.

For a moment a weird silence descended onto the room. I looked at Jula and she looked right back at me. There are moments in a marriage where the hard-earned telepathy of living with someone for years means no verbal agreement is needed. Jula's lovely brown eyes flashed approval, pride and sadness in a nanosecond.

"Yes, I can do that," I said with a wobbly lip.

"Good, I send you kit list and more info. We go Ukraine soon!"

Chapter 5

UKRAINE
DECEMBER 2022

THE NEXT FEW days were a frantic mix of nerves and excitement. Igor added me to the confidential communications software. When the kit list came through, I scurried about finding thermal tops, beanie hats and bits of ski gear that might come in useful. The dress code was dark clothes, but nothing military. It sounded vaguely like an invitation to a fancy-dress party, functional outdoor without looking like a PMC mercenary. The aim, to be as hard to define as possible. If you look ambiguous, mean business and are not a tabard clad NGO type, most people in a war zone will leave you alone. Closer to the frontline not everyone is your friend. Green and black kit may create enough ambiguity to be given a wide berth by those who might seek to take advantage. The dress code was in fact as much psychological as it was practical.

I did have a moment when checking my old sleeping bag where I thought, really Will? Are you sure this is a good idea? My parents had bought me the bag as an early Christmas present before I deployed to Iraq 20 years before. On my safe return to the UK, it had been cleaned and stored away. The stowage had been a strange moment of thanksgiving and also an act of finality. My military days were behind me. I was home safe, and that had been enough. Wrapped up in that bag were memories of nights under mortar fire, massive fatigue and fear. Here I was, an older man, volunteering once more for that uncertainty. Unwrapping that bag again.

DAY 1

THE DAY OF departure was a very cold and frosty morning. Jula helped me with my rucksack. For a second the magnitude of what I was doing overwhelmed me. The front gate seemed that bit harder to open. The nervous shuffling of heavy kit along an icy path made me feel weak and unprepared. The taxi driver was already lifting my gear into the boot. It felt like he had already denied me the chance to change my mind. I looked into Jula's eyes. In that instant you must find words that do not tempt fate. Words that say everything but also accept the reality of your destination. A strange romantic legalese that explains your deepest love without ignoring the possibilities. This must and always will be the very hardest part of heading into a war zone.

The taxi driver stood at a respectful distance as we hugged each other. I watched Jula waving in the street until she was a little dot against the white frost.

"You are crazy man going to Ukraine," said the driver in English.

"Maybe, but we must help all we can," I replied with the programmed fluency of a politician.

The driver laughed cynically. "You be home for Christmas."

"Which one, Catholic or Orthodox?" I laughed. The driver grinned in his mirror as if to indicate, touché.

As the vehicle climbed to higher ground it was clear that there had been quite a heavy dump of snow. Pulling into my destination, it was hard to discern house numbers with great folds of snow Christmas- carding everything. Eventually we found the right place. On leaving the car, a miserable blast of cold air rattled my clothing. My morale dipped. The sudden gale symbolising how far from my comfort zone I had strayed. Lifting my kit from the boot, I was met by Michal.

Michal was one of those people who just instantly gifts warmth and confidence. My nervous face must have been the give-away as he ushered me into his kitchen and placed a lovely milky coffee in front of me. A security professional by training, he could tell immediately that I needed information and reassurance – not necessarily in that order!

I told him how nervous and frightened I was, and strangely this made him relax more than ever! He had been expecting a hardened military professional. Clearly much had been lost in translation. Having run operations into Ukraine before, I think he had had his fill of Walter Mitty types who wanted to show off their specialist knives and kung fu credentials. My bookish persona would not challenge his expertise and authority and I could tell he appreciated that! No martial arts chat from me.

Michal kindly and clearly explained what the mission was. He made it sound like an extraordinary road trip rather than a journey into a war zone.

We were to head to a location, collect a convoy vehicle, head to another location, collect supplies and then rendezvous with the rest of the convoy near the Ukraine border.

The drive across Poland was a stark reminder that it is a big country! We drove all day, till the winter sun began falling behind us, an orange and yellow arc reflected against the endless snowscape as we headed ever eastwards. There was something almost magical in the gloaming that evening. A vista that a John Masefield or C.S. Lewis could have fashioned into an Art Deco Christmas tale. The Wolves really were running.

As darkness enveloped us the snow began to fall in great,

ridiculous flakes. Supersized crystals were soon blocking all but the wipeable areas of the windscreen.

Sometime later in the blizzard darkness we passed a massive monument. A looming monstrous object appeared, completely filling the view from my side window. The area behind the structure was a black void, which seemed to absorb any ambient light. I went from thoughts of Art Deco fairy tales to the reality of an Art Deco nightmare. Majdanek Camp. A place of unspeakable suffering - a Nazi death factory responsible for the industrial murder of thousands in the Holocaust. A shiver ran through me. I remember suddenly feeling a very long way from home, the current situation somehow serving to remind us that such horrors are still with us.

The road was becoming harder to discern, the snow all but obliterating signs and landmarks. The blessed sat nav at least gave us an impression of the road, approximate warnings of junctions and bends. To keep our spirits up, Michal and I talked about everything. Home, family, life, no subject was off limits. Working in security Michal had for many years provided close protection for Sting. We both laughed when one of his songs came on the radio.

"The boss is listening," I joked.

In the distance a faint glow penetrated the storm. Our big rendezvous. I became very nervous as we approached the emerging truck stop. A new level of reality was kicking in. I had grown used to the warm little micro world of our cab. We parked up and approached the other vehicles. The snow was knee high in some places. Straight away Igor came bounding over, making introductions and sharing jokes. The team were an extraordinary mix of people, veterans, athletes, one dancer – all united in the snow by a common cause, and the cold. Once again, the instant kindness of strangers caused my nerves to vanish into the winter winds. My only concerns now were the extreme weather and how much ketchup was dripping off the hotdog that had been thrust into my hand.

Once introductions were over the convoy running order was confirmed. Coffees and teas were chucked to one side and we were off towards the border. The snowstorm had thankfully eased off. Before long we were racing past a long column of traffic which stretched into the distance. It became clear that we had joined some form of NGO/aid fast track toward the border. Others it appeared would have to wait for hours to cross into Ukraine.

The border was very businesslike and well run, checks were speedy but thorough. It was a similar experience on the Ukrainian side. Once on Ukrainian soil the mood changed somewhat. Communications shifted from mobile phone to our own radio network. On clearing Ukrainian customs, the fun chatter was reduced to call sign updates. The feel was very reminiscent of driving at night in Iraq.

I said as much to Michal. His response was very reassuring – just remember that everyone here is on your side! There is no insurgency. Sounds silly to say but at the time being able to remove the fear of IEDs (the waking nightmare of Iraq) from my thinking made me relax massively. After a very dark drive we arrived at our base at two o'clock in the morning. The base was very impressive, self-contained, secure and very much what would be termed by the military as a Forward Operating Base or FOB Reveille was to be at 6am and getting into my old sleeping bag I allowed myself a little moment of thanks that there was at least no sentry duty.

DAY 2

IN WHAT SEEMED to be a nano second, I was awake again and people were already cutting about and preparing breakfast.

Everyone approved of my tea. Personal kit packed and ready
to move, we were put to work straight away, re-packing and
loading. Within five minutes I was more than aware of how
woeful my fitness was! Huffing and puffing, I seemed to have a
knack of finding the heaviest kit to carry. They cut me a bit of
slack when someone mentioned to the assembled helpers that
the English bloke was in his fifties, slack which was quickly
revoked when we were joined by Jacek who was ex-Polish
Navy, ten years older than me and lapping me on the box runs.
The shame of it.

As the last vehicle was being packed, an alert came
through stating that our region was under missile attack. A
heavy dose of adrenalin washed through me. Imagine that fear
sensation you get when forced to hard brake in a car. Imagine
that extended beyond a few seconds and your brain enters a
new level of consciousness. Time seemed to stand still. I felt
simultaneously hyper-alert and hyper-fatigued.

The convoy veterans quietly went under hard cover
with all the drama of a well-rehearsed corporate fire drill.
We waited till the all clear, defusing the tension with silly
stories and jokes. Air defence had clearly worked their magic
and the alert ended. We all slapped each other on the back,
bonded by the uncertainty and the strange elation of a shared
experience. Survival is a strange instinct. Survival as a group is
an empowering one.

Following the 'all clear,' we were straight out of the gate
and on the road. First stop was a children's charity. The cold
was biting. The wind so strong it induced pain in the eyes
and numbed faces. I was very glad to get stuck in and unload
the vehicles until I was ushered into one of the rooms where
boxes were being stored. There in the corner were some orphan
Ukrainian children sitting around a solitary laptop. When
they looked up at me their eyes were just so unbelievably sad,

I had to quickly stack my box and leave the room. My bottom lip was wobbling, fighting back the shock of witnessing such unexpected, silent, innocent suffering. Our donations suddenly felt very insignificant.

Heading back down the corridor I managed to hide my tears. "Just keep grabbing boxes from the truck," I kept telling myself. Thankfully the howling wind was causing everyone's eyes to water. Or maybe everyone was crying too? You would have had to have had a heart of stone not to be moved by those little bobbly hats and utterly lost little faces. I felt rage too. In that moment I would have gladly burned Moscow, laughing as I danced on Russian bones.

Once the delivery was complete, the children appeared in the doorway to say goodbye. One shy little girl peeped from behind a carer. I would like to think she gave me a little smile. More lip wobbling on my behalf. In truth I was a little worried. If I was going to be this tired and emotional on the first drop the next five days were going to be tough. Was I as mentally prepared as I needed to be?

Next drop was body armour and thankfully I had no bottom lip issues. This time food issues! The recipients of our kit were just lovely people and they insisted that we stay for lunch. Igor thought why not, a quick snack?

We were ushered through to a room and there before us lay a feast which completely covered a very large table. Hungry after the morning's lifting and shifting, we all tucked enthusiastically into the food. I felt very full and slightly concerned when a second course emerged, even more concerned when a third course arrived. You can imagine how we were feeling when a very large cake landed on the table, massive slices were doled out to each of us. We must have been eating for around three hours.

What a strange and emotional day - yet fascinating

talking to everyday Ukrainians who were now fighting for their lives, young people who had suffered tremendously and were prepared to do so until victory. We all appreciated that in feeding us they were clearly sacrificing their food, their precious electrical power and that was in of itself very moving.

The next stop was a warehouse, run by a very jolly Ukrainian team, whistling and joking. Ignore the equipment involved and it could have been a warehouse anywhere. For them the war was the warehouse, and the war was totally normal now. The clanking forklifts wrapped in tired tinsel carried our heavier goods into trucks heading straight to the east.

From the warehouse we moved on to an academic institution. The academics were really working hard in support of their students at the front, many of whom were now in Bakhmut. Passing through the very grand main entrance we found lecturers, ground staff and all manner of helpers grafting away in support of the war effort. Despite the laughter and good humour, one could not help but feel the tremendous sadness of it all too. Here we were in what had once been a thriving seat of learning. The alumni were now at war.

Many of the students who had at one time taken notes in the seminar rooms where we were now delivering our supplies were either dead or wounded. The lecturers reminded me of those Edwardian academics like the great M.R James who struggled to keep schools and colleges running during the First World War, preserving their institutions in the vague hope that when it was all over everything could return to the previous normality. Then as now everyone privately knew that nothing could or maybe should ever return to how things had been before the war.

Despite my musings there was an intoxicating positivity to all the endeavour around us. Looking at the academics, it was clear that whatever their respective views and disagreements were before the invasion, everyone was now on the same side. They now existed in a new world where practicality trumped theory. Necessity had eradicated faculty politics and previous concerns. Petty politics is very much a peace time privilege. A great cause had brought their society together in a way that made me feel weirdly envious.

The lecture halls were now full of helmets, food, boots and all manner of kit. Again, despite my musings, it was all surprisingly jolly, rather like a military jumble sale. There was time to snatch interesting chats and insights into Ukraine as we stacked equipment and I got my breath back! The only young people we saw were all in uniform and there were lots of them. Think of a scene from Second World War London and that would give you an approximation of the civilian clothes/military uniform ratio in this town.

As a semi-comedic aside, on leaving that institution a Ukrainian soldier saved my life. I slipped at the top of some very steep icy stone steps. I had resigned myself to an inevitable nasty fall when a powerful hand grabbed my jacket and held me whilst I found my footing. I weigh 120kg (Yes, I know), so this gentleman must have had some serious upper body strength and lightning reactions!

"Close!" he said in English, chuckling before disappearing into the darkness. I saw the rest of the team looking at me laughing too.

The final work of the day was back at base. We were met by the CO of a local company of Ukrainian soldiers, who were to collect some of the military kit donated by UK veterans. What a great bunch of lads they were, very switched on, very funny and deeply moved by the support from the UK. I cannot tell you how thrilled they were with the British kit, particularly the waterproof Gortex. The thought that people from so far away were thinking of their welfare induced a few Ukrainian wobbly lips too. They all spoke amazing English and it was fascinating to hear about the lives they led before the war.

I got on very well with one lad who had been working in software and was now an NCO. Less than a year ago he was designing apps and websites for companies all over Europe, now looking at his gnarly hands and living-in-a-ditch demeanour you could see that he had changed beyond his years. Looking at the faces around the room they were all so very young. I could see how they were also enjoying simple things like sitting in a comfy chair and flushing toilets. Funny what you miss when your life is turned upside down.

Suddenly it was time for them to go and - a bit of a recurring theme in Ukraine - they just disappeared into the darkness as thrilled as kids on Christmas morning with their new kit.

We had a quick evening meal – debrief regarding the day, planning for tomorrow and lots of banter. Then sleep.

DAY 3

ANOTHER REVEILLE IN brutal military fashion. Waking up in that sleeping bag was grim two decades ago. At least the aches and pains had gone by the morning in those days! Igor wanted to move - no time for hanging around, ablutions, breakfast, kit check, then out of the gate.

The weather was appalling with near blizzard conditions. Fortunately heading south, the weather improved a little and the countryside opened up into a vast expanse which those who had travelled across the US said reminded them of the mid-west. We drove across this endless landscape all day; other convoys would overtake ours and there was much waving and thumbs up. Soldiers driving past would wave and throw up victory signs. At least I hope they were victory signs. The feeling was we are all in this together and together we will win.

When we stopped for fuel, I would find myself marvelling at the brand-new garages – often brightly lit (they had fuel for generators, I guess). Inside the garage shopping area, everything seemed fully stocked with crisps, cola and all the usual healthy eating travel fare. The seating areas were comfortable and brand new. You could have been at any motorway service station anywhere in Europe, until you looked at how everyone was dressed, which reminded you that this was as much a military rest area as a service station.

The day was turning to night when a grid reference arrived on the secure communications. Our next drop was to be a bit out of the way. We detoured off the MSR (Main Supply Route) and onto a pitch dark miserably bouncy road - the sort that clatters your fillings and will either exacerbate or cure any bad backs. Fifteen minutes later, grid reference found, we paused in the darkest dark I had been in for some time. No ambient light, just the sound of a winter wind and the gentle throbbing of powerful engines.

As if by magic a torch flashed towards the ground about 50 metres from us. A woman about my age in military uniform emerged from the darkness and directed us to a collection point. I don't know why but I imagined she had been something like a librarian in her civilian life. Once our vehicles were parked up from nowhere personnel arrived out of the void to help – directed by the "Librarian".

In the darkness I suddenly found myself shaking hands with the local commander, introduced as the Brit who had come with all the gear donated by the UK. He was eager to convey his massive thanks and to make sure that I could see where it was all going. Many items like boots, socks and helmets were re-issued straight away. To the person reading this who donated the chain saw, I particularly remember that being handed out to an exited soldier. They knew that the chain saw was on its way and for it finally to arrive had made this chap's Christmas. Off went the chain saw back into the darkness.

Drop complete, we were back on the road. Our final work of the day was to deliver the UK civilian kit to the relevant depot. The tents and sleeping bags were most welcome and again I sensed that these items were issued directly to those in need. Same with the dog and cat food. I suspected that many of the depots closer to the front line live "hand to mouth" in the charity sense – not very much gets stored. Kit arrives, it's unboxed, it's distributed.

I was expecting to spend the night in a sleeping bag on a roll mat, so it was a very welcome surprise to discover that a local hotel had offered to put us up for the night. We were fed with amazing steak kebabs and given a pint of local beer. We all went straight to sleep.

DAY 4

ON THE ROAD we saw the early morning sun break the horizon, bathing the Ukrainian steppe in a spectacular orange glow. The scale of both land and sky seemed very different. The normal daylight rhythms of a wintery Northern European day changing as we headed south. The climate becoming noticeably more temperate, more early autumn than mid-winter.

That afternoon we were joined by our military escort. Close to the front it is not advisable or permitted to drive around without guidance. The risks of freewheeling and straying within range of the Russians are very real and make for bad headlines.

Our escort led us to a base where we delivered generators

and related ancillary equipment. The atmosphere was palpably different at this location. Its proximity to the enemy was not lost on any of us. The soldiers were infused with that strange laid-back fear that permeates all front-line places. In essence, no one worries about silly things anymore. You save your energy for the real dangers.

We were invited to eat with the soldiers. This was a great honour. Feeding takes on massive significance in a war zone. Mealtimes provide a break from the hard physical work, a chance to sit down for a while. It is a precious time where in-jokes are shared, horrible experiences are diffused, and legends are born. The fact that we were trusted enough to be invited into this inner sanctum of the soldiers' world was a privilege and testament to the impressive conduct of our team. We feasted on roast chicken, cold cuts, pasta and all manner of pickled things. Just to listen to the stories, witness the exchanged, knowing glances as a collective horror was remembered and shared was extraordinary and deeply moving.

After lunch a new route had to be selected. In frontline areas a road that was safe in the morning can become a killing zone by the afternoon. Once Igor was happy with our new coordinates, we continued to motor east. It was clear that we were much closer to the front. We started to see massive damage and destroyed vehicles; huge lumps of steel twisted into incredible shapes.

Several hours later we were at our final drop of the day. This proved to be quite a complex delivery as it involved delivering tons of medical equipment and the retrieval of refugees and their pets. Once parked up I noticed that there was no one around (think Covid lockdown but with real mortal fear). I could see that many of the surrounding structures were exhibiting the strange damage that artillery can inflict on buildings. One rather attractive mansion house on a terrace seemed to have had half its foundations blown away from under it but appeared to remain standing through a sort of cantilever effect. Other buildings remained untouched save for a dual aspect hole puncturing a corner room.

At this location we were cutting around at about twice the speed of the previous drops. The cold evening air felt supernaturally heavy with a sense of danger. An inexplicable animal sense that just being here represented a new level of risk.

We were met by a chief surgeon who came and told us that our deliveries were literally saving lives. He was very much the weary leader, and it was clear that everyone who came out to help had been living under sustained stress. They were still extraordinarily kind and hospitable but there was a notable hardness and strength there too – they had seen it all. You could feel the rage coming from them. I suppose when you have lived as they have had to do, you become very focused on how to stay alive. Suffice it to say having spoken to some of the locals there, the Russians had better watch out for the next hundred years.

Once the helpers found out I was English, a Ukrainian man came up and wanted me to pass on his thanks to the UK for looking after his family who were now safe in the West Country.

"What a wonderful country the UK is. Never forget that," he said, gripping my hand as if I had forgotten it. My bottom lip started wobbling again.

When the refugees arrived, we helped them across to our vehicles and began placing their pets in the special animal rescue vehicle. This caused massive distress as I suspect that this was the first time that some had been separated from their dogs and cats after the horrific bombardment that they had been through together. These people had come from the very front line and were obviously traumatised. The yelping of the dogs and yelping of the people was sometimes indistinguishable.

We were preparing to leave when the chief surgeon asked if we wanted to go out for a meal as it was the least he could do!

I must be honest and say going out for a meal was absolutely the last thing on my mind! Our natural survival instincts were saying, Let's go, let's go, it's time to leave!

Before I knew it we were piled into vehicles and roaring through unlit streets, making full use of the war zone highway code. Do not stop for anything. It was so dark it could have been the middle of a field for all I knew. Screeching to a halt we bundled out of the vehicles and were ushered into a sort of end of the world version of Pizza Express. A mad and wonderful meal arrived – some of the best pizza I have ever had. The atmosphere in the place was electric – it was the world cup final, but the real buzz was that here we all were sticking two fingers up to the Russians and having a Sunday meal with our new friends. The place was filled with the natural warmth and kindness of people who just want to live and enjoy the moment. They were great fun, and that meal is a wonderful memory.

What about the refugees I hear you asking? They wanted to stay in our vehicles, to them the location must have seemed incredibly safe compared to where they had come from. On our return from the mad pizza place, they smiled patiently and began settling in for the long journey. The two women in our vehicle were your classic elderly Slavic ladies, replete with headscarves and straight out of central casting. I suspected they were old enough to remember the last time total war had come to their village.

One of them reminded me so much of my Polish Babcia,

same grim determination matched with quiet resignation. The other lady was a retired English teacher who told me that the two of them were trying to get to Denmark, she had a daughter there. I think these two had been surviving behind the Russian lines before the recent advances. It was bottom lip time again as I thought of what they must have been through, of how difficult it must be in your late eighties to leave everything you have known and travel thousands of kilometres into an uncertain future. What a way to spend your last days, living in total fear.

Later that night we swapped vehicles. My new role was to drive drivers who needed to sleep – it made sense at the time. After about half an hour of my driving I looked over and noticed my Polish Naval friend, Jacek, eyes wide open and staring at the road.

"I can't really sleep," he said.

"It's quite normal," I replied. "The stress and adrenaline of the last few days will play havoc with your ability to relax."

He suggested that there was another reason, my driving! I admitted to him that I am not the best driver, having only passed my driving test fourth time around. I had also not driven for nearly three years and that that was on the other side of the road.

"That doesn't worry me," he said. "You need to move further to the left."

I respectfully suggested that in the absence of road markings and cat's eyes, I was choosing a line which did not lead us into the path of the endless trucks which thundered past us going the other way.

He calmly nodded and said, "It's just that the locals tend to leave discarded mines and UXO very close to the roadside."

Immediately I moved a foot further to the left, and with that my Polish Naval friend drifted off to sleep.

In the early hours of the next day, it was my turn to sleep. My driver this time turned out to be the Polish journalist Mateusz Lachowski who had joined our convoy for Polish News. For Mateusz think a young Jeremy Bowen or Fergal Keane. To some people he had become the face of the Ukraine War on Polish TV.

I asked him where we were going now, and he said that he was heading to Bakhmut - after he had left me with our convoy. He laughed heartily as the look on my face must have been priceless.

It was fascinating to talk with Mateusz about the risks he takes to bring the stories from the very front line to the world.

"What are you doing after Bakhmut?" I asked.

Mateusz responded that he had a couple of things to do in Ukraine and would aim to be home for Christmas – he made it sound like the most normal week ever.

Finally arriving at our destination, I thought I must phone my wife before we settled down and had our usual four hours of sleep. Seconds into the call the air raid warning sounded.

"What's that?" Jula said.

"Oh it's some form of alarm, nothing to worry about."

At that moment Jacek said loudly that he had had enough of shelters and was staying in his sleeping bag. My wife heard everything! Talk about timing!

DAY 5

EARLY START – but not as early as previously. Also, our hosts treated us to an English breakfast. The last thing I was expecting in rural Ukraine! The plate of bacon and eggs was gracefully placed in front of me. The waitress gave me an expectant look, hovering as though I was working for

Michelin. I gave them a hearty thumbs up, my perceived expert approval making their day. Everyone agreed that an English breakfast was a wonderful thing. I mentioned that there were also Irish, Welsh, and Scottish breakfasts too.

"What are they like?" asked Jacek, keen to expand his breakfast knowledge. I told him that because of Brexit he would never find out. I thought it was funny.

First drop of the day was a location whose commander reminded me so much of a teacher from my school that I had to do a double take. I could not get over how well organised this place was. As we unloaded, it was amusing to be told, "Just dump it there by the Javelins." The lifting and shifting continued. I noticed our two old lady refugees helping too! They were frighteningly strong.

I was vaguely aware of a van screeching up close to our vehicles and a soldier saying something about a dog. My Polish was good enough to pick up little bits of Ukrainian. The upshot was that members of his unit had found the dog wandering around in a daze near a family home which had been completely destroyed (along with the poor family) by Russian artillery. Someone had told them that a group of Polish dudes (and one Brit) were rescuing animals. This chap had driven a considerable distance to hand the dog over to us.

The poor dog looked absolutely distraught, head down and shaking. It was one of those moments where I could see that taking the dog was not just about saving the animal. It was also about hope. Out of something as horrible as finding a vaporised family, knowing that the family pet at least could be rescued, would be a major morale booster for this bloke and his chums too. We made space for the little fellow. Lots of hugs all round and back on the road.

Another massive drive along an endless highway. The winter sun cast a mysterious light across the fields and domed churches. The beams refracted through ice and frost cast a nostalgic magic across the land. I felt a yearning for happier times, for a genuinely peaceful Christmas. The old ladies traded stories of Christmas past and their lost world. Legends of sadness and hope.

Hours later we arrived at another dark town. The old ladies were delivered to some form of reception centre as were the pets (only the really distressed dog from Donbas remained with us). Thankfully, I was tasked to another location and did not see the Babcias leave. That saved me a major bottom lip moment. It's amazing how close you can get to people in 24 hours. I hope that they are OK. It would be lovely to think that they are in Denmark now, safe and sound.

Long day completed we went for a meal – massive amounts of food again. We were joined by some Ukrainians who we had met earlier in the week. The power was out. We ate by very dim light but what a meal of laughter and shared experiences. An evening I will never forget. There was a strong sense of Christmas and that intangible, shared yearning for a past that you know can never return. Departing in darkness we arrived back at base in time for a brew and sleep.

DAY 6

OUR WORK DONE, the plan was to head straight for the Polish border. However, one of the vehicles decided to play up. There were major issues with the electronics. We found a local mechanic who set to and over the next few hours pretty much rebuilt the vehicle.

While we waited, we chatted with the locals and were asked into someone's house where we were fed and looked after beautifully. We could see how difficult life was for them without power but the whole community was looking after each other with all sorts of rotas and systems worked out for cooking and homework and so on.

Vehicle fixed, we were ready to go with two extra passengers – our Donbas dog and a lady whose husband was receiving specialist heart surgery in Poland.

A quiet drive to the border saw us arrive almost at the head of the NGO queue – blocked only by Deutsche Welle. "Who are they?" asked someone. "German Telly" I replied. They were soon moved.

The head of customs then invited us into his offices for a Christmas drink and a thank you for all we had done for Ukraine. Igor politely explained that we were all driving.

"Who isn't driving?" demanded Colonel Customs, determined to have a drink with someone, anyone!

The team pointed at the Brit. Before I could say anything, everyone's shots were tipped into a tumbler. I found myself holding a glass full to the brim with brandy. Igor indicated that I should down it. National pride at stake, I wolfed it down. It felt like one of those mad dares you can only get away with when you are nineteen. It wasn't long before I was feeling pretty groggy!

Once through the border checks, it was more open road again. I was out of it at this point. At least my diplomatic drink had rendered me officially unable to drive. I awoke at a motorway service station just in time to see the Ukrainian lady reunited with her family and then we were off again. I finally made it home about 3am. As I stood by my gate the street was well lit and peaceful. The Christmas lights seemed bright and innocent. It was hard to believe that I had been away less than a week. The gate lock clicked in its familiar way.

What just happened? I thought.

Chapter 6

FEBRUARY CONVOY

THE COLLECTION MOMENTUM continued into the
New Year. By the end of February another load of equipment
had been assembled in the UK. There were boxes of boots,
helmets, rucksacks and Bergens to be collected and delivered
to Ukraine.

Gregor arrived in his cathedral-sized van for the next
stage of transportation. I am still not quite sure how you are
allowed to drive a van that big on a normal licence but that is
one for the DVLA! He was quite shocked at the amount of kit
waiting for collection.

"There you go," I said. "There must be about 500kg of
equipment there!"

Gregor looked at me shaking his head. "Try 1000kg," he
said.

As we heaved box after box into the van, I began to
suspect that Gregor was right (later I discovered he was almost
spot on 1000kg). Van load completed, the stolid Gregor set
off for Poland. I have to confess at this stage that I was not
travelling with him as I had some "day job" stuff to complete in
the UK.

As the great pantechnicon pulled away, I shouted to
Gregor that my flight was departing tomorrow evening.

"That's when I arrive the other side of the channel," said
Gregor.

"I'll race you," says I, joking.

Gregor's face told me that he accepted the challenge, and he roared off into the night. Never challenge a Polish van driver to race a plane. It's not fair on the plane.

Gregor arrived in Poland only about six hours after I did. The heat coming from his engine told a tale of almost time-travelling levels of hard driving. I had visions of Gregor racing along under my plane, cursing the sky and whipping his van! The man is a legend. Next stop was Igor's depot.

After a quick coffee and cake (morning cake is still a big thing in Poland, as is afternoon cake to supplement the other four meals of the day), Igor and the gang emerged from the various store sheds, and we began unloading the van. They were very impressed, so impressed in fact that Igor was already on the phone to the various charities and units we were supporting in Ukraine, letting them know what had just arrived from the UK.

Igor turned to me. "You want to go again?"

"To Ukraine?" I asked. My wife was standing right next to me. The situation was almost a repeat of last time I gave her the lost puppy look.

"Go!" she said laughing.

At that moment Jacek (of December run fame) emerged from the back of Gregor's van and said: "Good, you are coming with me."

Three days later I climbed into the legendary "Green Hornet" van (one of the team's vehicles). The van had at one stage been some sort of municipal mobile workshop, painted in an energy sapping municipal green, hence the "Green Hornet" reference. For the interior, think a well-loved but well-organised garden shed. I bid a nervous good morning to Jacek. We were joined by a very cheery Ukrainian lady who was heading home to liaise with several children's charities.

Heading off into the winter sun, this trip felt a bit

different, maybe more relaxed in some ways. I had got to know
Jacek quite well over the last two months. We share a similar
sense of humour and more importantly share the scary habit of
singing while driving.

We had pick-ups to make in Lodz and Lublin before
heading for the Ukraine border. I had never been to Lodz
before, an industrial town located right in the heart of
Poland. Lodz is a gentrified, grimy mélange of factories and
warehouses, some converted into expensive apartments. Mix
a Birmingham and Manchester together and you are getting
there. The dark satanic mills of Lodz are located all around the
historic site of an even more dark satanic industry. Genocide.
The Lodz ghetto and associated rail yard. The Nazis had forced
Jewish people into ghettos (a Yiddish word for quarter or
neighbourhood) before being transported into the murderous
camps. The Lodz Ghetto was infamous.

Parking our van, we collected equipment from a building
literally on the other side of the road from the Lodz Ghetto
memorial wall. Tourists were beginning to arrive as we stacked
the van. Our Ukrainian passenger looked at the wall and then
looked back at me as if to say – will we ever learn? I looked
at the wall and looked back at the lady. I was soon to discover
from her the answer is very clearly no.

As the journey progressed the Ukrainian lady began to
tell her story. In the early days of the war, she was living in the
Kherson Oblast. She described how the scale of fighting and
invasion was at first stupefying, the initial disbelief paralysing.
Everyone thinks that they will know what to do in these
situations. The truth is without reliable information you cannot
even tell where it is safe to run. In the ensuing panic many
innocents drove into the enemy, dying in a hail of gunfire.

The lady described how she managed to get hold of a
minibus, filling it full of children. At one point she realised

they were driving along a contested road, finding themselves in the middle of a massive fire fight. To watch her describing this was an extraordinary experience. It really did not matter that my Polish was poor. The well-remembered stress and fear in her eyes told its own story. She went on to describe how rounds from small arms struck the vehicle on many occasions. Somehow the minibus held together and kept going. They seemed to be protected somehow or so they thought.

She then broke down in tears when she described the moment shrapnel hit her vehicle and removed the jaw of a passenger. I tried through my twisted seatbelt to comfort her as she mimicked the look of total incomprehension and fear on what was left of the face of the child they were trying to bandage. She was completely reliving the moment. A sudden shriek came from within the woman's body, a noise of primal frequency, a necessary expulsion of negative energy. I believe we would have screamed like this before we had language. It was truly shocking just being with her. This level of remembered trauma began to have a catatonic effect on the lady.

To be honest I was not sure what to do. Jacek was driving and had his watery eyes on the road. I tried to be as understanding as I could. This is the point where language becomes a terrible barrier, grief blocking the communication skills of the sufferer. My Polish was not good enough to offer the level of consolation she needed. We were momentarily reduced to our primate roots, relying on facial expression, sounds, and eye contact in place of the complex empathy afforded by language. Other than offer her a flask of sweet tea, I was useless.

Eventually she began to breath her way out of the memory, the stress deflating as she very courageously calmed herself down in great lung busting spasms. Silence descended upon the van. For what seemed like an age the only sound was the drone of tyres on the road and passing cars. I felt powerless to say anything. I am sure Jacek felt the same.

"Anyway," she said through muffled sobs, "we made it to safety."

The delayed conclusion to the horror story came out of that long silence. Arriving almost out of context. I dared not ask about the wounded child.

The border was not far away now. The roads seemed different and unlike what I remembered from the last crossing. Jacek said that we had been told to try another route. This border post seemed brand new and more automated than the crossing used in December. This will be a doddle I thought. If you can jinx something with a thought, then I certainly did it that night. We joined a queue with just one other vehicle. There were in fact no other vehicles around at all. No other people either, completely unlike the other border crossing which was rammed night and day.

Jacek and I got out of the van and wandered around a bit (something we were not supposed to do but in the absence of anyone official we took the opportunity to stretch our legs). We were joined by the driver of the solitary vehicle behind us who seemed equally bewildered by the situation. Here we were, held up at a massive border post that seemed to be deserted. The other driver and his colleague had come all the way from Barcelona to deliver aid. Lord knows how long they had been on the road. They were remarkably chipper in the face of a biting, freezing wind and no information regarding when they would cross.

Three hours later the border posts flashed back to life. We were beckoned forward. It was as though the last three hours had never happened.

"They must have been on a break," I quipped.

"Or more important deliveries were being made," replied

Jacek cryptically, with a knowing smile. Military supplies must take priority.

We passed through the Ukraine border without further incident and trundled off into the pitch darkness that was Ukraine at night.

DAY 2

THE ROADS WERE empty, and we were able to motor along with ease. We all decided that the chosen border crossing was a mistake and we reported as such back to Igor. It also left us with a longer drive to our base. Much quality grumbling followed which is always good for morale and then best forgotten.

Ukraine at night was a strange place to be. The power blackouts caused by the Russian infrastructure attacks created a preindustrial darkness only our ancestors would have known. All you could see was the extent of road ahead exposed by your headlights. The buildings and villages emerged out of the darkness. Only revealing snatches of architecture at the last minute, rather like those vast images of the Titanic suddenly looming into view at the bottom of the ocean. It made it very hard to get a sense of place. It would have been easy to think that Ukraine at night was just a series of brightly-lit petrol stations emerging from the void every 20km as luminescent islands, only to disappear back into the darkness.

We arrived at the base at the statutory silly o'clock in the morning. It did not feel quite right to be the only people there (two other Traczer team groups were heading for different locations). I hate rattling around places particularly if you are used to them buzzing with people. Childishly, I kept my head torch and reserve torch very close to hand. Not sure why the dark bothers me so much when there are plenty of real dangers to worry about in Ukraine. Securing the vehicles, we went straight to sleep.

About four hours later the lights buzzed on. That terrible plinking buzz that anyone who has been in dormitory accommodation will know and love. A merciless sound that seems to amplify fatigue and sap morale. Our interpreter had arrived and was already munching breakfast. I on the other hand was about two socks and a thermal vest behind in the getting dressed and getting on stakes. Thankfully Jacek is a little more laid back than Igor and my tardiness was forgiven.

Breakfast completed, it was straight out of the gate. First drop of the day was one of the warehouses we had visited before. Last time I had promised myself that I would do a few stretches before unloading but that never happened. Even before the van had come to a halt, the pallets were down and we were dropping off nearly two tons of supplies.

The pace was relentless, and it was clear that the demand for our cargo meant there was no time for chatting. No sooner was one pallet completed, it was wrapped (with that industrial strength cling film) and wheeled away into the cavernous warehouse. After a frantic hour we were done. Finished in every sense of the word. Jacek and I held onto each other gasping, while the foreman came out to say hello and goodbye. He looked just like Ronnie Barker in the "Four Candles" sketch with a similar level of misunderstanding. Between my dreadful Polish and his dreadful Polish, we managed to establish something of a rapport. He even allowed us a little peak into the warehouse. I could see why they were so busy. I may even tell you why one day.

Waving goodbye to Ronnie, we drove and found some hard standing tarmac to re-pack ready for our next drop. At this stage we had picked up a trailer of cot beds for the military and in typical hurry up and wait fashion, the beds had to be moved from the trailer to the main van and the kit in the main van to the trailer. By this stage Jacek and I were both earning our grumbling merit badges. Swearing, whinging and cursing our way through heavy lifting and trapped fingers. Weapons grade complaining any soldier, sailor or airman would have been proud of.

The route to our next drop took us past some smashed up and destroyed buildings. Life instantly and demonstrably gutted from these streets. I suddenly felt very guilty about my previous grumbling. As we passed fresh, unnaturally empty spaces, an old man was standing outside the remains of a house. He was staring blankly into an unfathomable distance. His was a nightmare of a face, wiped of hope while contemplating a private abyss. An abyss no doubt being repeated right across Ukraine that morning.

The relief of reaching the next depot was the antidote we needed. Hard practical work perfectly fills the gap that outrage creates in your heart. The adrenalin and negative energy thankfully dissipated by the strain of lifting very heavy kit. Again, we were loading pallets. We must have looked a sorry sight. Jacek and were I struggling with some ridiculously heavy equipment.

A group of lads took pity on us and came rushing over to help. I could tell they were saying words to the effect of, "Look at these old bastards!" "Come on, Grandad!!"

Every pallet we loaded went straight onto a bigger truck and almost before that truck was full it was pulling away, such was the demand for essential supplies. War is a very hungry beast. The level of consumption is quite different from peacetime. The gentler considerations of peacetime time-keeping and economising give way to the constant rhythm of send it now and send more. To wait would mean death for those the supplies are destined for. Or defeat.

FEBRUARY CONVOY

The relentless logistics were exhilarating to watch. The churning pace of trucks arriving, married with a dizzying carousel of forklifts, shouts, laughter, abuse and departure again before one even had the chance to think. I leant against some pallets and tried to catch my breath. Two very young lads approached and asked Jacek and me what we were doing. We must have looked to them like the oldest and strangest men in the world. Watching their faces as we told our story, I could see that our presence as foreign helpers confirmed just how much their lives had changed in a year. None of us thought eleven months previously that we would be shifting tons of kit in a warehouse supplying the largest European conflict since the Second World War.

We confirmed and reconfirmed this fact back to each other again and again, as though formally registering our respective disbelief and solidarity. Some of the stories the lads told us were grim. Some were humorous. It was that gallows humour which creeps into wartime existence, the safety valve of laughing along with the horror or at it. Jacek talked of a bridge he had crossed in the opening stages of the war. It was blown up fifteen minutes later. Had he stopped earlier for an intended break he may well have been destroyed along with that bridge. These stories of chance and escape were met with nods and the shared gratitude of survival.

To add some British levity to proceedings, I announced to the group that I had lost weight since the last convoy. In order to prove my point I jumped on the pallet weighing machine (probably the only thing that would take my weight), and to Jacek's mild surprise I was now 111kg. 9kg lost in 7 weeks. No one was impressed. In the eyes of the group, I was still a lump. The two lads said that they wanted to see me under the 100kg mark on my return or else. For a happy half hour break you could almost forget you were in a war zone.

Next and final drop was a roadside collection. The vehicle was already waiting for us as we pulled up into a quiet lane alongside a graveyard. Unloading the van, I could not help but notice the flags waving as a very sobering reminder of the terrible price Ukraine is paying for its freedom. The people we were delivering to were cheerfully fatigued. After quick hugs, we set to with loading. Suffice it to say, these people had come from a kinetic place and had that noticeable crackle of controlled stress about them. They just wanted to get moving. You would have thought that a bit of respite in a rear area would be welcome relief and maybe it was, but these people wanted to get back to their base and distribute the equipment as soon as possible.

In less than half an hour the van was loaded. Before they left, they gave us a bag of apples that they had found in a building. It was a lovely gesture because that was all they had. There was something very sad about that as we watched them motor off. A little shiver went down my back as I thought about where they were headed to.

So far on this trip we had got away with not being fed by kindly locals. However, we had made the classic operational mistake of staying in one place for too long. We had been seen. You guessed it, we were invited into someone's house for a meal. As with our previous visit the food was copious and delicious! They were so kind to us and it was a shame we had to leave but we needed to get back to the border. The "Green Hornet" was needed back in Poland to pick up more kit and head back to Ukraine again with another convoy. Our Ukrainian passenger reckoned she knew of a better border crossing, however it was not the crossing we had agreed to use with Igor. It also meant a much longer drive. She was adamant though that her crossing was quicker and after a bit of discussion we thought – well, she is from Ukraine she must know!

Chapter 7

APRIL CONVOY

AS GREGOR, JULA and I pulled into Igor's Polish depot we were met by the usual crew. They were already opening the truck before Gregor had applied the handbrake. This time the UK donations were really something to behold, the veterans of ARRSE, Cheltenham College and the people of Chedworth had truly surpassed themselves in terms of donations. We now even had our own UK storage bay allocated to us – which we very nearly filled.

As we prepared to leave, Igor called me (he was at a fundraising event) to say thank you and ask the question; did I want to come with them again? I was on "hands free" so once again my wife heard everything.

"We are going to the Donbas this time" I am not sure whether "Donbas" registered with my wife, but it certainly registered with me.

"I will call you tomorrow about body armour and helmet." Igor ended the call abruptly (in that busy Alpha male-type way) and I climbed back into the van.

DAY 1

I KEPT LOOKING back until my wife became a waving blur and the taxi turned down a side road. This convoy was not going to be like the last one. The previous friendly warehouses and banter with the lads would have to wait for another trip.

The taxi driver could see I was a bit on edge and asked if I was going to Ukraine (my lucky old army Bergen was a perhaps a personal security fail). I confirmed that I was and he told me not worry.

"It's only the Donbas that is really dangerous at the moment."

What he meant was, no one is mad enough to go down there right now. I said nothing and thanked him for reassuring me.

Once at the RV my co-driver arrived. Anatoliy was a bit of a legend in the group and only two weeks before had had a tough experience extracting his team from Bakhmut. He was definitely a no-nonsense Ukrainian, complete with that impressive combination of kindness and hardness that is very much a facet of their character. He gave me a massive hug and thanked me for everything that the UK had been doing. The conversation was difficult as he spoke little English but fluent Polish. My Polish was being strained to its very limits, but we understood each other enough to have a laugh and settle into the journey. It is amazing how a common cause can make up for language issues.

Before we headed for the border, we needed to collect gear in Poland. The first stop was a huge medical supply centre. The location was a major operation supplying a range of charities and NGOs. The staff and visitors were all either Ukrainian or Polish. Once they found out I was a Brit I think they forgave my woeful language skills. Over the din of forklifts and crashing pallets I managed to make myself understood. We were collecting wheelchairs and rehabilitation equipment specifically for soldiers (I suspect not a typical collection).

One curious lady asked where we were going. Anatoliy shot me a glance. I answered Ukraine.

"Yes, but where in Ukraine?" asked the lady.

I replied, "Just across the border."

Anatoliy looked at me again as if to say, well done. Clearly, I had passed his Mark 1 operational security test! In locations like this even though chances are everyone is on the same side, one must always be mindful of who is listening.

Back on the road again, our next RV was at a motorway service station. Equipment was delivered to us in a quiet corner of the car park. I had met the man before, and he greeted me with a knowing, almost conspiratorial nod. Very little was said as we loaded the kit. We were on our way within five minutes.

It was a beautiful early spring day. Evening arrived, delivering that very specific sunlight of the magic hour. The sunset lit the table-top flatness of Eastern Poland as far as the eye could see. For some strange reason, the vista reminded me of long continental drives on family holidays. I thought about asking Anatoliy, "Are we nearly there yet?" but recent experience had taught me that much of my humour does not always translate in the Slavic world. Besides Anatoliy is not someone you want to convince of your stupidity. I also knew we were nowhere near being "nearly there."

Igor was on the net and rearranging our next RV. Within the hour we were all together, sitting with coffees and reacquainting ourselves. We were also joined by a journalist who was going to film our convoy. I liked him immediately as rather than film he was helping us reload and tether trailers like one of the team.

Before we left Anatoliy's son arrived to have a few moments together with his father. Glancing at them from a polite distance, it really brought home the quiet daily sadness and pain of separation that many Ukrainians have had to endure. Anatoliy beckoned me over to say hello to his son who gave me a massive hug and then started speaking perfect

English. He was able to correct some of the more alarming misconceptions that my terrible Polish had created over the last few hours. Anatoliy seemed mightily relieved. Apparently, I had been confusing the words "pregnant" and "heavy" in Polish. I went bright red. Lord knows what the ladies at the medical supply depot must think of me!

Igor indicated we had better gear up and go. We still had a three-hour drive ahead of us just to reach the border. Anatoliy's son hugged me again. We promised to go and watch Man City together one day. He knew where we were going. He looked at me and without saying anything, I knew he was worried for all of us. I left him with his father – I cannot fathom what these moments must be like for Anatoliy or his son. A terrible mixture of pride, fatalism, and love. I will throw endurance in there too.

As we drove away, I looked back at his son and waved. I thought of waving in a similar fashion to my wife hours before and wondered what she was doing. For a moment I also wondered what we were doing!

Before the border we stopped to refuel. We were ahead of the rest of the convoy for reasons unknown but may well have been because Anatoliy drove at Bakhmut speeds almost all the time. I checked my watch to make sure the time/space continuum had not been irreparably damaged by our careering vehicle. We sat quietly and waited.

I discovered that Anatoliy is a bit of an expert on honey and that there is actually a honey season. The honey revelations came on the back of a radio report about honey flavoured sugar flooding the European market. We were having a very interesting chat about bees, Clarkson's Farm – Ukrainian beekeepers….when, Knock knock knock.

I looked out of the window and a very irate garage attendant was telling us to move.

"You are not allowed to park here!" he yelled.

It was 10.30 at night and there was no one around. We were parked in an area away from the forecourt disturbing nobody. Or so we thought. Anatoliy explained very calmly that we were waiting for the rest of our convoy and then we would soon be on our way. He could see we were heading for Ukraine, but this martinet was having none of it. I remember he looked rather like the chap that does the travel writing for "The Guardian." A ridiculous situation was developing.

Thankfully and as if by magic, Igor and the rest of the tribe appeared as the garage man was about to kick up a gear in the jobsworth stakes. The other vehicles took a pump each and Igor indicated for us to do the same. As all the pumps whirred away, we were racking up enough Zlotys to be customer of the day. I headed with the journalist into the mini café and started explaining loudly in English what I thought of old misery guts hiding behind the till. The man looked very sheepish as Igor covered the bill. I attempted to stare the man out Paddington Bear style. Grrrr. I caught the journalist and Anatoliy smirking, and realised that it was me that needed to wind my neck in.

Back on the road, we were at the border in no time. Past the last chance Biedronka (a strange mix of Sainsbury's or Waitrose with a smattering of Lidl) and we were already thundering past the massive queue of vehicles heading into Ukraine. When it comes to border crossings Igor has perfected that delicate balance of acting with the arrogance of champions while maintaining a very disarming charm that is essential not just to bypass the conventional column of traffic but the NGO column too. On my last run in "The Green Hornet" I realised we were just too nice and too polite.

We were through the border in under an hour and back on the road in Ukraine. I remember *I've had the time of my life* from "Dirty Dancing" came on the radio. This was notable, as before, there had been no commercial radio signal. I also noticed all the lights were on. During my previous two visits, Ukraine had been a bible black nocturnal world of dipped headlights. Now everything looked quite different. Ukraine felt different. We even passed a kebab van. There was a palpable confidence in the air.

We were not staying at our usual FOB on the first night. Parking the vehicles, we were led to our temporary accommodation and very quickly found bed spaces and prepared for sleep. Igor was feeling a little bit under the weather. I gave him a Lemsip and very shortly we were all sound asleep.

DAY 2

AS USUAL, WE were up very early. Breakfast was a massive cauldron of borscht and lovely fresh bread. I did not opt for the raw garlic garnish. There are some things I refuse to eat at 5.00am. Without the raw garlic, borscht is not a bad start to the day and after a couple of bowls I was ready to face anything.

Leaving the temporary accommodation, we headed towards our FOB. This involved a short drive through a town that had previously been relatively quiet. The place now seemed to be buzzing, chemist shops were open, delivery men were arriving, and it felt like the sort of morning you would see in any market town. There was a sense of confidence too, in the way people walked and in the conversations in the street. Just like the lights at night, Ukraine had clearly entered a new phase of the war.

It was the same when we got to the FOB. The FOB was benefitting from what I term the "Bastion Effect" (Camp

Bastion being the base in Afghan that grew eventually to be the size of Reading) I discovered that there was now a proper gym area and a sauna! I resisted the temptation to "big time" it with the journalist and say, "When I first got here, the best you could hope for was the luxury of a sleeping mat and a sleeping bag." I checked myself as I realised there are people who work out of the FOB nearly all the time. My once every six weeks trips made me nothing more than a gifted amateur... at best!!

The Bastion Effect was further confirmed by the fact that no sooner had we arrived it was time for a NAAFI break. Lovely fresh coffee was produced and the dark tea they love in Ukraine. To see their faces as I put milk into the tea was something I wish I had photographed. I might as well have been adding Coca Cola to a single malt. An interesting cake was produced too – made of compressed sesame seeds and formed into a nougat-like block.

"Nougat?" I asked.

No-one seemed to have heard of nougat and from the blank looks coming from everyone in the room I backed down. I was still worried about the pregnant and heavy word confusion from the previous day and hoped "nougat" did not translate as some Ukrainian or Polish obscenity.

Before I had had a chance to drink my coffee, Igor jumped up and it was time to move. One thing I have learned recently - a key bit of kit is my thermos mug. On receiving orders to move, take the red-hot drink and (rather than waste it) tip it into the thermos mug, screw the top back on and drink it later - usually, hours later!

Once outside, Igor guided me over to a monster of a four-wheel drive vehicle. The beast sat there in the yard like a vehicle from a Mad Max movie. I could see that said machine was directly descended from one of those sturdy late 80s early

90s Japanese four-wheel drives. Igor explained that it was
being donated to a unit in the Donbas. He then proceeded to
show me a picture of the smashed and smoking remains of its
predecessor.

"You drive to Donbas. Do not worry, both survive, in
hospital now."

I felt hugely reassured.

The journalist was going to be my co-driver. The engine
growled into life. Whatever combustion solution existed
in the belly of the beast, the engine was clearly tuned way
beyond factory specifications. The tyres were great Tonka-like
monsters. The sheer noise of this creature would have struck
fear into the heart of the toughest environmentalist. We took
our place in the convoy and were soon on the open road.

As we headed down through Ukraine that confidence
that I mentioned before was absolutely in abundance. We
would stop to refuel, and you could just feel from soldiers and
civilians alike a very positive and almost happy energy. Having
survived the winter, a very specific form of spring was clearly
on the way.

The journalist and I sang and swapped stories all day. We
must have looked quite mad as we flew along singing 80s
classics and talked politics (often at the same time).

"I wonder what's in the back of this truck?" I asked at one
point, slightly annoyed with the lumpy object that dug into the
back of my seat. The journalist was driving and registered my
feeble attempts at shifting some extraordinarily heavy items all
wrapped up in heavy black plastic.

"I think it's best we don't know," came his sensible reply.
I stopped immediately. I did not want accidentally to press
something that might really spoil our journey.

After a long all-day drive, we arrived at our
accommodation and were immediately invited to eat with

some local dignitaries. The meal was delicious and arrived in an endless procession of platters and bowls. I chatted at length with the boss of a local agri business who had an exceptional knowledge of the UK and the challenges faced by UK farmers! I did say to him that I thought that currently Ukrainian farmers might be facing a few more challenges than their UK colleagues. He waved away my concerns, saying that the land would be cleared of UXO very quickly and crop yields would return to normal. I did not doubt it for a moment.

Inevitably the vodka began to flow, and many toasts were made. The lovely words spoken about the UK and the support that arrived from afar brought back my wobbly bottom lip (which had yet to make an appearance on this trip). I was also asked to make a speech which Anatoliy very carefully translated. I don't think I said anything about "pregnant" or "heavy" but it seemed to go down well with the local politicians. As the meal came to an end, we all hugged, and the bottom lip wobbling returned as they wished us well and to stay safe. They all knew where we were going. I could see that even for Ukrainians a trip to the Donbas was a very big deal.

DAY 3

ANOTHER NIGHT ON a hard floor with just a sleeping mat was actually working wonders for my back. I had the strangest dream. People from my childhood, long since dead, came to say hello and find out what I had been up to. At one point in my reverie, I found myself reminding a friend of my grandmother that her husband was also no longer with us. She apologised for forgetting such an important piece of information. I awoke to find myself feeling strangely reassured. Answers on a post card, please. Memento mori?

After a quick breakfast, we were back on the road. The

further east we went, the more you could feel the war. Early
in the afternoon we arrived at our first destination. We were
dropping medical supplies and equipment. The loading area
of the location was guarded by a group of lovely old boys who
looked just like the Ukrainian version of Dad's Army.

As with Warmington-on-Sea's finest it would have been
a big mistake to underestimate them. Their senior NCO
waved us to a halt and scanned our vehicles. He was taking
no chances. You could just tell that whatever happens in the
future, one thing is certain, no-one will ever gain access to his
car park without the express permission of his Dad's Army.
Not even Zelensky. When the time comes for demobilisation,
I predict that there will have to be serious negotiations
before they hand over control of the car park. For a moment
I thought that we were not going to be allowed access, but
once we opened up the trailer and one of the medics arrived to
confirm who we were, Dad's Army were all sweetness and light
and up went the barrier.

I must also say that in emptying the trailer those old
soldiers worked incredibly hard. In under fifteen minutes we
had emptied tons of wheelchairs, walking aids and other kit
from the vehicles. We had a good laugh racing each other,
trying to push overloaded trolleys up wobbly ramps. They
were lovely chaps, the youngest was probably in his late 50s.
Without a doubt if they could have gone to the front they
would have done. They were just too far north of the necessary
age barrier. You could also tell that the truth of this really hurt
them. Their uniforms hung off stiff old shoulders and it was
impossible to disguise the obvious bad backs and rheumatic
legs as they staggered under the weight of our deliveries.
However, they were doing their bit. This location was their
frontline and they worked and protected it with all the passion
and dedication displayed by their younger colleagues in the

field. Very honourable men. Their service meant younger men could be released for front line duties and wounded men would quickly receive the donated medical equipment.

While we were packing up the trailers a group of civilians arrived looking for Igor. A family who had been robbed of their washing machine earlier in the war had arrived to collect a brand-new machine donated by a Polish family. I had no idea we even had a washing machine with us! Dropping the tail gate we gingerly edged the machine to the lip of the trailer. We then lowered it to the ground in a manner which went completely against all health and safety lifting advice. I staggered backwards and painfully stood up straight. I caught the eye of one of Dad's Army who nodded and grinned as if to say, "You are about five years behind me, mate, tops!"

There the washing machine shone – a brilliant white monolith in the spring sun. The family stood in silent admiration while the father manoeuvred his van closer to the machine. Suddenly their little boy broke free of his Mum and jumped on top of the machine.

"I hope the Russians don't steal this one!" he yelled, and everyone laughed and clapped.

He was a very sweet little chap, and somehow his innocent and truly joyful outburst served to exorcise what had clearly been a terrible year for them and their community. The fact that everyone could laugh about it was both cathartic and a huge indication of the Ukrainian character and strength. While Igor posed for a photo with the boy and his Mum, I stood to one side with the boy's Granny who was laughing with tears in her eyes. She hugged me and thanked us for everything. Big wobbly lip time. I saw the journalist filming and thought, hold it together, Will, hold it together! Even Dad's Army were sniffling.

We departed the area having made many new friends.

Despite everything, what a tremendous feeling of strength and solidarity.

At the next location Igor and Anatoliy were meeting with the Ukrainian Army for a full briefing and to pick up our military escort and minders. To venture into the Donbas without them would be monumentally dangerous.

The journalist and I were able to go for a little walk. People were starting to commute home. A man was having a haircut in a barber shop across the street, two young lads were buying a bottle of Coca Cola and a big bag of cheese and onion crisps from the store next door. All the lights across the town were now on, and everything felt almost normal. We could have been in any other European city at dusk.

It was the acoustics that I noticed first. Eerily and suddenly the noise of the street changed forcing me to look up – or rather through this terrible gaping hole in a block of flats. Although the destruction was weeks old, you could still smell the dust and the burning. All normality evaporated. To see and smell such damage in person is frightening and humbling – the scale and depth of the destruction cannot be conveyed on TV. Also, the weird juxtaposition of unscathed apartments only metres from the void. In the window of a fully lit kitchen, I could see the inhabitant draining pasta and preparing to settle in for the evening, presumably as he must have done when oblivion missed his home by the width of an average car.

Igor was on the comms and wanting us back in the vehicles. We had a long drive ahead of us. We were now very palpably heading towards the front lines. Only the military could be seen. One was suddenly very aware of little civilian activity save for the odd battered transit van or G-Wagon NGO convoy.

Our vehicles fell silent. The Ukrainian Army minder was on the comms with his unit arranging an RV to hand over

ARRSE donated kit. As far as risk was concerned, we were now through the looking glass. You could feel it. I was not even aware at the time that we had passed the border and were in the Donbas. A maze of roads and lanes gave way to a strip of wooded area. I could see military activity. It was time to leave the vehicles. We had already had the brief about staying on the hard standing and five and twenty metre checks. From now on, do as you are told, when you are told. No photos unless we say so.

The journalist and I stood by the vehicles as soldiers emerged from the wooded area.

"It looks just like on the telly," I found myself saying (I wanted to take it back before I had even finished speaking).

The journalist shot me a glance. And then a smile. We were all a bit sacred in our own way. I was more than a little relieved when we opened the relevant trailer and started unloading the boxes. Nothing like having something to do when you are a bag of nerves.

Our UA minder introduced me as the UK veteran who had organised the donations. It was a lovely moment as soldiers bounded forward to give me hugs and thanks. I have said this many times before and I will say it again, seeing the profound boost to morale that kit donated by UK veterans gives to Ukraine's troops is deeply moving. These lads and lasses now know that the Brits are thinking of them and that we deeply appreciate the terrible sacrifices that they are making. I felt so very proud to be representing all those veterans who had donated. Strangely, no wobbly bottom lip. I find it is the civilians that tend to activate the bottom lip wobbling phenomenon.

As each box was opened, soldiers were called forward according to need. Bivvy bags here, day sacks here, socks here etc. Battle buddies would find something and remind their chum that he needed a better helmet cover or point out that another set of mess tins might be useful for the section. It was amazing to watch, like disciplined, caring ants picking away at a carcass. All working together for the greater good. Even the empty cardboard boxes were repurposed. They make for comfy seating in a trench or, if necessary, can even become a temporary sleeping mat.

It was strange suddenly to recognise a particular set of boots, last seen a week ago in the fluorescent light of my parent's garage, being hastily tried on by a grubby warrior. In that moment, the Donbas seemed that bit closer to the Cotswolds. The delivery complete, it was big hugs, and for those who did not speak English a very intense eye contact of thanks. Then they were gone, back to their positions and we were on the move again.

All the time we were getting closer to the front. We stopped for a comfort break at one point right next to a pile of smashed and degraded Russian ordnance. A burned-out Russian APC sat half on half off the road, the Z still visible through the residue of smoke and oil. For the second time that day I found myself thinking, "Just like on the telly." Clearly, I have some deep-seated cognitive dissonance issues that need addressing!

Ukrainian soldiers approached our minder. Military tourism is not an endearing quality when you are tired and working hard. The minder explained who we were and everyone relaxed. A young lad approached me and spoke in an almost perfect English accent. We had a lovely short chat about history, hobbies and technology. Then it was time to go. It was a shame to leave my instant friend behind. Sometimes you just hit it off with people. He was so young, no more than nineteen.

On we drove into the darkness. There was no light, just

massive vehicles roaring along the highway towards the fighting. Those ancient Soviet-era trucks make an almost prehistoric sound. The combination of tyres and indestructible engines work together to make the most terrifying nightmare of a noise. A convoy of those beasts is a veritable psyops all of its own. They were not stopping for anything either. The speed they travelled was for the greater good and not in adherence of some peace-time highway code.

It was time to eat. Our vehicles came to a halt in a mud park that was firm enough to be navigable. The sticky dirt was a strange brew of diesel, water and the famous black earth of Ukraine. Head torches on, we followed the strong smell of woodsmoke and cooking food into a semi-subterranean log cabin. There before us lay trestle tables laden with food. We took our seats at one end and marvelled at the variety of bread, cheese and sauces, all of it fresh, nothing processed.

Great cauldrons of soup and stew were being lifted from ancient wood fired stoves by powerful old ladies in headscarves. The stoves flashed flame and sparks. The heat could be felt from a considerable distance. Each of those giant pots must have weighed at least ten kilos, yet the ladies moved them from stove to table effortlessly. Igor explained to me that these ladies had started a volunteer kitchen to feed and provide support to those heading up to and leaving the front lines. They wanted to provide their brave defenders with a home-cooked meal and a place that gave them respite from the pressures of the front.

At that stage we were the only customers and clearly something of a novelty being non-military. We were soon joined by a group of soldiers who had clearly just left somewhere particularly grim. They looked deeply tired and yet deeply happy at the same time. I expect the shack- dining room seemed like the safest place in the world compared to where they had been. They grinned at us through wind-burned lips and faces. As they took over the table it was hard not to stare and imagine what stories they had to tell - except they did not tell those stories. I had forgotten that the last thing front-line soldiers want to talk about is the front line. Now they could check their phones again, their concerns were, who is going to win the premiership, look at the picture Dima's daughter has sent, my car needs a new back windscreen. Normal stuff. I tried not to stare as they wolfed their food down. The soldiers were up and gone before we had even thought about finishing our meal, eager to return home and make the most of their leave.

A group of medics came in. They too looked weary but happy, more laid back than the Infantry who had just left. Igor engaged them in conversation. They chuckled at something I half understood, some dark humorous story which I think related to where we might be headed.

The journalist got me a cup of tea whilst Anatoliy raved about the fresh tomatoes. They were indeed very fresh and tasty. I am not normally a fan of tomatoes, but he had done such a fantastic sales job on them that I just had to try one. Truth be told, I was more encouraged by the fact that the medic's stories did not seem to phase him. Anatoliy had "seen the elephant" and I had much more faith in his quiet confidence (and experience) than duty rumours. Our UA colleague/minder also just listened and smiled. Meal finished, we got up to leave and thanked our hosts – they were such kind and brave people. What they are doing for morale and welfare in the Donbas is incredible.

DAY 4

ON WE DROVE into the all-consuming darkness. I had no idea where we were. It became quite clear that the lack of geographical information was quite deliberate on the part of our UA minders. Did it really matter? In terms of "the mission" we were tasked with delivering donations and equipment. Nothing else. We were now in the land of "need to know." Our minders needed to know where we were. We did not.

The vehicles came to a halt. Instant silence, save for the buzzing of my nervous system. Our minder whispered that we should leave the vehicles quickly and quietly. No light. No talking. Grab body armour, helmet and Bergen and await further instruction.

We stood apprehensive in the fresh night air. A solitary dog barked in the distance. Already the combination of helmet, body armour and Bergen began to pull at my aching back. That feeling of everything being heavier than your muscle memory allowed for. The kit began to tip me slightly off balance. I steadied myself on one of the trailers oblivious to the fact that we were now surrounded by soldiers. Where had they come from?

In the moon shadows I could see we were now surrounded by an indeterminate number of what Orwell famously described as "rough men," smelling of life in the field. A mix of bonfire, adrenalised sweat and diesel. These chaps carried the invisible weight of recent combat. You could just feel it. A lethal patrol. Even in the ambient light it was clear the working parts of their weapons were freshly carbonised and oily from constant usage. We must have seemed almost alien to them in our wobbly civilian ways.

Seconds later the most terrifying Alpha male in military history appeared and gave a whispering briefing in Ukrainian and Polish. But not English. I could just make out some of the "Actions on" instructions but not enough to really understand. This was more than a little worrying. We were on the move before I could grab hold of the journalist for a better translation.

From the moment we stepped off, the pace was that weird dance between a jog and a walk that Infantry types love to inflict on us less active mortals. The feeling was very reminiscent of a CFT that I had not prepared for.

My mind went back to my days in the TA and finding myself one weekend being rolled into a mixed group of soldiers who had yet to pass their annual combat fitness test. Mercifully in those days the TA CFT was only four miles carrying 20 kilos of weight. For a person of average fitness it was a challenge. For someone who found themselves in a pie- eating phase of their life the CFT quickly exposed any weakness.

On that occasion I rapidly became the focus of the PTIs' attention after about the first half mile. I thought I could wing it and was caught out. Thanks to me the squad began to "concertina." I struggled to keep pace as the PTIs raised and lowered the tempo in order to achieve the allotted time standard. Once the concertina motion kicks in the rhythm of the squad becomes harder to maintain. Anyone behind the offenders works twice as hard to catch up with the remainder of the squad once the pace is quickened by the instructors. I and one other candidate were moved to the rear of the squad and became the back stop of shame. It was not my finest hour.

Now in Ukraine I was Mr Concertina Man again. There were no encouraging PTIs this time. Although outwardly gracious I was very aware that I was really irritating the tired lads behind me. Within five minutes any remaining illusions I had regarding being a useful military being in Ukraine were long gone. My breathing was all over the place. I was really struggling to keep up and maintain my footing. Only a sweaty pride kept me vaguely in line.

Meanwhile the Ukrainian soldiers floated along with twice the load we were carrying. They had youth on their side and the wiry field fitness that comes with constant patrolling and surviving. The one positive was that I was so focussed in maintaining the pace that I did not have time to think about how close we were to the bad guys.

Buildings emerged from the land, massive block shapes, moonlit and foreboding. Our path cut through to a wrecked landscape, strewn with heavy lumps that were familiar markers to regular users. Hazards were indicated with sharp hand signals from our minders to prevent us newbies from crashing onto our faces. We moved quickly under hard cover and were led straight into a subterranean cookhouse.

Our minders disappeared and we were left in the capable hands of the chefs. A pork chop at two in the morning with a rather tasty gravy, washed down with NATO standard "Screech," seemed like quite a treat. As soldiers arrived from patrolling or other duties I was impressed by how accommodating and caring the chefs were, leg pulling where appropriate or quietly plating something up for a tired lad who needed a bit of TLC.

The cooks were very much soldiers first and chefs second. I talked to one who had worked in London and spoke perfect English. He knew all the lads and had that unofficial sounding-board, pastoral-care quality that can be invaluable in terms of morale. He was also that sort of cheerful lad who finishes a marathon round of pan-bashing, helps clean one of the crew-served weapons and then stags on sentry duty with a smile. They do exist!

One pork chop and rice pudding later (I noticed one of our lot dipping a Pork chop in the rice pudding!) we were joined by two seniors who talked us through what the unit had been up to. We were shown grim videos that made me rather regret wolfing the rice pudding. The unit's drone operators were clearly making life hell for the Russians.

It was bedtime. Igor and the rest of our group were allocated their own sleeping area. For some reason I alone was detailed off to sleep in one of the platoon dorm spaces. In total darkness (save for a little red light), I followed one of the seniors down concrete corridors, through sandbagged doorways, stepping over holes in the floor and jumping over missing stairs. I had no idea what sort of building we were in. Whatever the construction had been, the place was now a labyrinth of smashed corridors, detours, double-backing and strange echoes.

The sleeping area was a warm fug of gun oil and flatulence. The kit gave off that classic sweaty, garden shed, never-quite-dry-aroma of field life. Various long shapes squirmed and snored in the darkness, cocooned in their sleeping bags, movement limited by their cot beds. Bed spaces were laden with bandoliers and all manner of very heavy equipment needed at a moment's notice. The senior showed me a free bed space and asked if I was OK? "Lie down for four hours," was his version of a bedtime story.

Quickly I unpacked my sleeping bag, closed the Bergen and lay down. The room was hot and disorientating. Only seconds before I had been dog tired and now I was wide awake. The heavy snoring and bashing movements of the unseen sleepers was a little unnerving. In the dim red light, I could no longer see where my minder's bed space was.

Come on mate, sleep! I chided myself. The stress of not sleeping then developed into a much more worrying problem. I needed a wee. At first it was the sort of I can sleep, ignore this and pee in four hours time need for a wee. That did not last long. Within fifteen minutes I knew I could not wait till morning.

I tried to imagine where the senior was sleeping. All I could see were shapes and lumps. Waking every bed space until I hit gold would probably result in a field-beating of bone-breaking proportions. Some of these men were just back from the front line. They lay in those weapon-cleaned-then-sleep positions that only truly exhausted men can achieve. Being woken by a foreigner without a password or identifying insignia might just be suicide.

I lay back, the combined childish fears of the dark, being in a strange room and potentially wetting the bed, served to make me feel very pathetic. Then there was the simple business of the rather large war outside. It sounds very silly to say this now but the voice of a particularly diligent member of the DS who took me through basic training came to mind. He was the sort of instructor that even the other DS were a bit scared of. His family was the army. He was also the sort of instructor that detected even the most minor slacking. It could be three in the morning, stagging on sentry, all compo-belly and shock of leaving the sleeping bag. A clear starlit night, just you and the peaceful training area, your helmet comfortably resting on the iron sight. That sleepy feeling that only happens when you must stay awake. Eyes about to close....his voice would be there in your ear. It would be enough to keep you awake for the next 24 hours.

He was a fiend for putting us under stress and seeing what initiatives we could come up with in order to improvise and overcome the hardships of life in the field. It was excellent practical training, particularly for those reservists like me who did desk jobs and had little exposure to hands on problem-solving. Now in Ukraine it was getting dangerously close to "hands on" time again. I wondered what the DS solution was to busting for a pee, in an almost pitch dark room, no comms, no sense of place, no knowledge of where the bogs were? Improvise! Yes! I had a solution quite literally to hand! In an instant I was fumbling for my thermos mug in the Bergen. Thankfully empty and with a wide enough aperture (perfect for the dark) I began unscrewing the lid. I know the DS would have been proud of me.

Lid removed I began psyching myself up for the unthinkable. I imagined the sleeping senior suddenly awaking, then the respective sections waking, me standing there in the tactical red light of shame, Igor being summoned to vouch for my sanity.

Then, mercifully from the void came the sound of men moving as quietly as they could, but definitely heading in our direction. I held off on the thermos, carefully tucking it into my sleeping bag. Moments later, the first few of them were in the room. The weight of their CFO kit almost tangible as it was dumped into familiar spaces. Their red light seemed incredibly bright. I waved at them as though marooned on my bed space, which of course I was.

"Do you speak English?" I pleaded

"Yes, who are you?" answered the soldier in a manner that said I am very tired and you had better be on our side.

The patrol were filtering into the dorm and occupied bed spaces that were emptying with a quiet, well drilled acceptance of the slumbering shift change.

"I am a British man working with Igor, we have brought kit for your unit and I need to go for a wee wee."

I do not know why I said "wee wee."

For a moment the soldier peered into my face with a total lack of comprehension. I then compounded my self-infantilisation by saying "wee wee" again, this time in Polish.

For men who had just returned from blasted trenches and had probably taken lives in the last hour I must have looked like a very pathetic specimen indeed. I am sure that the last thing they imagined (as they headed in from patrol) was that a middle-aged Englishman in ill-fitting Helly Hansen would be asking them where to go for a wee wee.

APRIL CONVOY

The penny dropped (no pun intended). The soldier laughed and explained in Ukrainian to his colleagues what was going on, something along the lines of clean your weapons and get your heads down while I take this old duffer for a pee!

He then grabbed my sleeve and pulled me up in the manner of a Judo instructor volunteering a student. I dutifully followed him, shuffling my feet nonagenarian style so as to anticipate the uneven floor. He laughed and said that he better not hold my hand. Stifled giggles echoed in the abyss of darkness around us as we both acknowledged the ridiculousness of the situation. Once again it was up hill and down dale through this monstrous concrete world.

At one point we were stopped by a medic. By moonlight she had seen me shuffling along and thought I had been injured. She stopped us and was immediately hands on in that instant diagnostic fashion combat medics subconsciously develop in theatre. Seconds later, she fell about laughing as my companion explained the real reason for my shuffling. I stood there smiling whilst they composed themselves. My help the aged badge already in the post.

Eventually we reached the bogs. I was expecting a fly blown hole in the ground. What confronted me in that weird moonlight was a very respectable sit-down loo in the middle of a Cathedral sized space, completely incongruous in that enormous hall. The cistern was plumbed into a thin white pipe which in turn appeared to be plumbed into heaven. It looked like a piece of installation art that wins prestigious prizes and is then purchased by a trendy council for the price of a family home.

The soldier hung back at a safe distance. I am glad he did not time me. Suffice it to say no horse could have done better. I flushed and placed the seat back down to demonstrate my domesticated "New Man" credentials. The soldier then grabbed my sleeve and dragged me back to the dorm.

Heading back into the darkness, I thought that if someone had told me this time last year that a Ukrainian corporal would lead me by my sleeve fifty metres through a ruined Robocop factory (1987 version of course) to an art installation toilet close to the front lines in a war zone, I would have said they were mad.

Three hours later the senior was shaking me and before I knew it, I was awake, stuffing my sleeping bag into my Bergen in record time. Kit checks then up. He gave me a look as if to say, "OK, not quite the duffer reported to me by the last patrol," and then smiled. I followed him down to the sleeping area where all the others were. Past the NLAWS and firing positions. The grey morning revealed very young, determined faces, wedged into sandbagged firing positions and murder holes. We found Igor and the gang. It was good to see them.

Back in the dining area, it was hard to believe we had been there four and a half hours before, even harder to believe the same chef was there, more cheerful than ever.

"Don't you ever sleep?" I said as he ladled a healthy lump of porridge into my bowl.

"Never," he said, with a mad smile. "And I hear you don't much either!"

The tab back to the vehicles was strange in the unfamiliar daylight, the ground totally different to how I imagined it. Never give me a map. The seniors gave us big hugs. Today was going to be a busy day.

We were soon heading through a large town that was completely boarded up. No-one was around. Our UA minder was in total control of our movements now. In the grey daylight it was very obvious that we were close to the front. The only sound being the chatter on the net and the occasional acknowledgement of our call sign. We bobbed and weaved and were clearly avoiding any obvious routes. Occasionally we would stop and wait. I later discovered this was because the planned route was being shelled!

After a morning's worth of bumping over rough ground, turning down little tracks, back onto a smooth main road for twenty metres only to then turn down a former residential street for five hundred metres, it felt like we were in some terrible maze. I did not have a clue where we were! Eventually we came to a halt outside a nondescript building.

Once outside, the air was a strange mix of warm sun and dry cold wind. I remember thinking this feels like unfamiliar weather. Charity workers emerged from nowhere. Weary shadows of their former selves. We began to empty a trailer of civilian clothing, general supplies and pet food. Inside the building were a group of elderly people, some quite disabled, others relatively sprightly and able. The charity workers, despite their worn-out demeanour, were a cheerful bunch. They worked around their charges with gentle charm and knowing remarks.

"Are you alright there Mrs X, those new wheels on your walking frame make all the difference, don't they?"

"Mr Y, come on let's get you a coffee and some cake, yes, that's right they have come all the way from Poland to see us."

My bottom lip was starting to go.

Back outside and heading towards the trailer...crump, crump crump CRUMP CRUMP crump. I could feel the compression through the air and the impact through my feet.

"It was actually worse first thing this morning," said one of the charity workers registering my concern.

CRUMP......crrrrrrrrrrump...crump.

"The wind has changed direction, so it sounds a bit closer than it really is," said the worker again, clearly trying to

provide reassurance whilst helping me with the other side of
a heavy box. Forget the wind I thought! What happens if the
shells change direction?

Now I do not know much about artillery and the only
other IDF I have experienced was 20 years before when a few
120mm mortar rounds flew into Basra Palace. That seemed
like the end of the world back then. Suffice it to say whatever
the calibre of these shells, they seemed way more powerful
than my memory of those rusty old Iraqi mortar rounds.
Judging by the body language of the charity workers these
earth-shaking random impacts were indeed all in a day's work.
Apparently, this level of "incoming" was to be ignored. We
continued to empty the trailers whilst I did my best attempt at
appearing to be as cool as the charity workers.

When we had finished unloading, one of the elderly
ladies offered me a coffee and a slice of cake. Once indoors the
occasional thundering outside did not seem nearly as scary. The
false comfort of being undercover. If any one of those rounds hit
this building, we were all done for. A local priest arrived, and we
joined everyone in a prayer of thanksgiving for our safe arrival. I
am not sure if the priest said a prayer for our safe departure, but
I can assure you I made several on his behalf, just in case.

In no time we were out of the town and into open
countryside. The landscape and the roads were empty. We were
driving at the sort of speeds you can only drive at on a country
road if you know that the roads are almost traffic free. The
comms would bleep, instructions dictating that we turn left at
a wrecked farm, right down a road that was punching above its
weight as an MSR and back around that village in the lee of a
gently rolling hill.

Sometimes we would just stop and wait. On one occasion
the UA minder turned to me as guttural commands came from
a secondary device.

"Bad guys," he said in English.

Anatoliy began mocking whatever they were saying. The UA minder started laughing and between them they shook their heads as if to say, "Is this the best that they can do."

Through the adrenalin and an obsession with staying hydrated I suddenly remembered I was desperate for the loo. After the previous night's activity I was developing a bit of a reputation. With a bright red face I asked the UA minder if I could go for a wee. If the laughter induced by the Russians was the warm-up act, then clearly I was now the comedy superstar. The simple answer to "Is it safe to go to the loo?" is "No!" However, the false concept of safety in a vehicle versus safety outside is worthy of a whole dissertation of analysis.

"Go, go!" giggled the UA chap. "But stay on road, no field, no bush." He indicated an explosion with his hands.

I tentatively opened the vehicle door, scanning the floor for anything nasty. Stepping down like the first man on the moon, my foot reached for the ground. Looking at where we had stopped, the cover we were under and available hard surfaces, it did not take me long to realise that I had no option but to wee where I stood.

There can be no embarrassment in these situations. Then the wind changed direction. A massive gust blew between our vehicle and the vehicle behind, causing me to have an accident of catastrophic proportions. Above the general noise of the Donbas and the howling wind, an incredible volume of laughter could be heard. Fortunately my trousers were made of some super high tech rip-stop (hopefully drip-stop) waterproof material. That saved me. The laughter was another thing. For about five minutes I had rendered the convoy ineffective. Anyone passing by would have assumed some sort of mass hysteria. Worse was the fact that the journalist was filming at the time and had recorded everything.

The comms bleeped and we had to move. Getting back in the vehicle, both Anatoliy and the UA minder were instantly re-focused. Thankfully the trousers were almost dry. I may well write to the manufacturers and report my findings as field tested in the Donbas. Signed, one very grateful class clown.

Rolling through another deserted hamlet, we came across a column of men. They walked with that fatigued determination of battle-hardened troops. You could just tell that they had got very good at their job. I was reminded of hundred-year-old grainy footage of men trudging along some sodden Belgian road. We came to a halt by a soldier I imagined to be the senior NCO. Our UA minder began pointing at electronic maps, and from the look on the sergeant's face I got the impression that our route was about to change again. With much talking in low tones, grim nodding and a "best of luck, mate," our convoy changed direction again.

After another half hour of careful driving we parked under some trees that ran along a main residential street. There was no-one around. The only sounds were comms chatter and the occasional crump of artillery. To the right of the vehicles was a concrete channel ditch about two metres deep. Perfect cover should the crumps wander our way.

The journalist and I chatted and agreed that in peaceful times this town was clearly a very nice place to live. An old man appeared out of nowhere. He was peddling a bike and clearly had no idea he was in the wrong gear. The agony of his huffing and puffing was enhanced by the cow-horn handlebars which he struggled to grip. More crumps in the distance. The old boy cycled on oblivious. I am absolutely convinced that despite his age he could have walked quicker than he was cycling.

A solitary Ukrainian soldier then appeared in the street.

He walked briskly with two see-through carrier bags, both filled with crisps, banana milk and chocolate, the sort of morale boosting rubbish you need in theatre. The soldier nodded and wished me good morning in English and disappeared off down the road.

"How did he know I spoke English?" I asked the journalist. He gave me a look as if to say, are you really sure you want me to tell you?

"You have a Union Jack patch on your fleece." The mystery was solved.

An escort arrived to take us to the casualty station. On arrival we were met by a very jolly surgeon who brought her exhausted team outside to see us. My vehicle was met by a MERT who were really keen to get their hands on all the FFDs, Israeli bandages and other emergency kit we had brought.

The senior NCO in charge of the MERT took Igor and myself round to the back of the ambulances and we immediately began to replenish the vehicles. The medic team worked out that I was that funny old Brit who had been bringing UK veterans' kit over to Ukraine.

One of them called me over to look at something. He handed me a helmet which had been brought over on the last run. I half recognised it: a PASGT type Mark. On initial inspection I was not quite sure what I was looking for. The medic's light red finger, dyed with disinfectant, pointed to a tiny little hole in the side of the helmet. It looked like a pencil stab through a piece of card. Nothing remarkable. You would not have seen it unless you were looking for it.

"The round entered here and travelled around the back of his helmet," explained the medic. "It then left the helmet and carved a furrow down his back and came to rest in the flesh of his backside."

The medic looked and me while Igor filled in the bits I had missed in translation.

"Thanks to whoever donated that helmet, the bloke lived. Weaker helmets just don't take the power out of the round."

The words hung in the air as the medic chewed his lip and stared off into space. The reality of that little hole in the helmet was somehow more impactful to me than the crumping sounds of the wider war and more frightening. I thought of that injured soldier. I saw him maybe relaxing a bit in his trench, turning to a mate. Snap. Snap. Then staring at the sky, wondering what had happened. Something wrong with his back. Shouts. A funny burning smell. The medic searching him for wounds, reassuring the soldier as his mates returned fire and arranged the casevac. I held the helmet up. It was heavy. A quiet and inert reminder of where we really were. More importantly it brought home the life and death impact that our donations can make.

The medic clapped me on the arm as if to say, "C'mon, we need to empty these boxes." The bandages were needed now. The MERT were going back out on the ground again soon. A large pack of old school (but new) FFDs were picked up by one medic, clearly a favourite bit of kit for him. Despite their obvious fatigue, the team displayed the weird energy of tired efficiency. It was almost as though their exhaustion made them better medics. They would probably tell me to "F off" if they read this but that is how they seemed to me. Battle fatigued will power. If you were wounded and alive when this team reached you, then these guys would save you. They had that magic feel about them.

Once finished with the ambulances, we helped the casualty- clearing medics with the kit meant for the station itself. For some reason they would only allow us to carry the kit half-way to the building and then would take it off us. I had a particularly heavy box and a young lad (who looked like the actor Jack Black) insisted on taking the box from me.

I said, "No, I can take it," but he really blocked my way. He just gave me a look as if to say, "You don't want or need to see what's in there." I let go of the box right away, feeling he had done me a tremendous favour.

Our UA minder was indicating we should leave. Too much time spent on the ground in one place is never a good idea. Our force protection escorts guided us back the way we came and then out onto a fairly good main road. They stayed with the convoy until we reached the edge of what they term "the military area." We stopped for a few photos and the senior NCO in charge of the MERT came and gave me a big hug. He looked me in the eye and simply said, "Thank you for coming, thank you for helping" I felt so very guilty that we could leave while these guys had to stay.

With that the military escort turned their vehicles around and were roaring back into the zone. I later found out where we had been and a little shiver ran down my spine.

Back on the road that deep tension across the shoulders fear began to dissipate. I had the sense of coming out of a trance and I suddenly felt very tired. Adrenalin only works for so long. After a short drive we saw the dining hall from the previous evening and Igor suggested we stop and have a break. In the daylight the surrounding mudscape looked bleak but busy. The journalist handed me some hot sweet tea and we hunched up on a table and began to fathom the last 24 hours. Not easy. Instead, I found a tasty loaf of crusty bread and began to make cheese and onion sandwiches. The journalist looked disgusted.

"What? You think it's OK to eat raw garlic at 5am!" I protested. Raw onion and bread is positively fine dining compared to a garlic breakfast.

We were heading north again and away from the "military

area." We had a long drive ahead of us. Late that evening our hosts greeted us like long lost family and then (you guessed it) ushered us through to a landscape of food. We were definitely hungry but this was going to be a challenge, soup, chicken, pork, fish. I did my best. We all did. Then came pudding. Then cake. We slept very soundly that night. I have had some hard days in my life but I think Day 4 of our journey was something I can never forget.

DAY 5

WE WERE UP early and fed the most delicious scrambled egg. Back on the road we were beginning to lighten up a bit. I think the tension of heading to, being in and returning from the Donbas had been underestimated by all of us. Certainly by me.

We were soon at our final delivery point. Here we were met by some very cheeky chappies who were real Ukrainian "geezers." They had a lot of stories to tell. After dropping off the last of the donations we were lead into a shed which I think was their sort of HQ.

Once inside, one of the geezers threw various items onto the crumbly concrete floor. He looked up at us like a cat wanting approval. There by my feet lay a greasy, smelly, mucky battle vest. Next to it lay a helmet with two telltale holes in the side. I picked up the helmet. It was as light as a feather. The total opposite of the donated helmet from the previous day. The plastic dome was malleable and cheap. Probably cheaper than the Russian camo pattern helmet cover. My hand was holding the helmet just below those two holes. Suffice it to say I rather wished I had not picked it up.

The man rooted around and pulled out what I thought was a home-made piece of ghillie-flage. It turned out to be a shredded battle vest of the same Russian model as the other one.

The wearer would have been equally shredded. The man grinned as we shook our heads. Grabbing the more intact battle vest, he pulled out the ballistic plate. It was not a ballistic plate. I doubt it was capable of stopping anything more than an angry word. If you are familiar with those hard plastic baby's bibs, the ones with the trough at the bottom to catch all the food, then that approximates the material the plate was made from.

Aside from the plate, the vest itself was of very poor construction. Poor stitching, poorly designed. Clearly that was now of no concern to the previous owner, or many others like him. The Ukrainian dude looked at me as if to say, "Don't be weak and feel sorry for these fuckers." As we shuffled out of the shed I felt very grateful for the hand sanitiser my wife had insisted I take with me.

We had one more task to complete that day before heading home. The handover of the terror weapon four-wheel drive. No tax, no insurance, ready for war! There it stood in its filthy matt coloured craziness. The vehicle was being collected and driven to another part of the front by a wonderfully courageous man who was the same age as me. Sacha. He had given up a very lucrative career and settled family life in order to defend Ukraine. He probably could have wangled a cushy job flying a desk for the army. Instead, he had chosen to get as fit as he could and push himself through basic training. That must have been tough for a man in his fifties. He passed his special to arm training and was now about to drive to the front line. He gave me a sad smile as he reversed and headed out of the gate. With one ripping roar from the engine he was gone. Truly a Hollywood moment.

At the time of writing Sacha is engaged in some of the most bitter and bloody fighting in the Donbas. An incredibly brave man and patriot. The fate of Ukraine is being determined by men like Sacha.

Chapter 8
JULY CONVOY

DAY 1

AS HE LIFTED the deceptively heavy body armour into the taxi, the driver looked me up and down and got back into the vehicle. I hugged my wife. The rituals of leaving for Ukraine now felt very much a part of our lives, the feeling of separation reminiscent of my boarding school days - that reluctance to return, balanced with the reward of seeing my friends. I looked back down the hill until I could see her no more. The short journey to the RV passed without comment.

On leaving, the taxi the driver looked at me with tears in his eyes.

"You go Ukraine?"

I nodded.

Out shot a firm hand. "You are hero," he said.

"I'm just going to help, I'm only there a week."

"Not matter, you are hero!"

The driver's bottom lip was going. Now my bottom lip was going. I was hoping to have zero bottom lip moments until we at least crossed the border. It was not to be. Now my eyes were welling up and we both hugged. It turns out he was born in Ukraine. He drove off with a salute, leaving me sniffling in the humid silence of a very hot afternoon.

I contacted Igor to confirm my arrival at the RV and was told to wait for collection. When the transport arrived, we were joined by a Ukrainian lady, Oksana, who would be travelling with us for the first leg of the journey. Her story was a shocking one. In 2014 she had been in her Donbas home when there was a click/flash. Regaining consciousness, she found herself covered in shards of glass. A Russian shell had destroyed her home. She had been running from Russian violence ever since, moving ever westwards until she found herself caring for Ukrainian refugee children in Poland. She told me this story in the matter-off-fact way that many Ukrainians do. Abnormal is the new normal.

Pulling into the depot I could see familiar faces cutting about. Busy waves and smiles. Anatoliy was pumping up the tyres of another Mad Max monster vehicle. He glanced up and grinned as if to say, "Look what I found!!"

Igor gripped my hand. "You drive this," he said as he handed me a gnarled lump of keys. The tyres were truly awesome with off-roading teeth for treads. The interior was for the scrap heap and caused much mirth as I attempted to make myself comfortable.

"No AC," quipped Anatoliy. "Old school AC," quipped Anatoliy again as he demonstrated that the electric windows actually worked! I felt so much better. 34 degrees outside.

Time to go. The engine of the beast dragged the frame forwards without any encouragement from me. A mechanical wolf in sheep's clothing. It would take all my limited driving skills to tame this one. Once on the open road the roar of the motor cleared a path Moses would have been proud of. Sweating executives thought better of cutting me up or even attempting to overtake me. Never have I driven such a beast, designed for war rather than the motorway. I would be a liar if I said Donbas Diesel Monster was not an ego boost. In the roasting afternoon sun, for a fleeting moment, I was the road warrior.

That is until a myopic yellow Fiat 500 sailed out in front of me. A bad time to discover that my brakes were not completely on speaking terms with the tires. Creaks and scary noises shuddered through the vehicle. Thankfully, I managed to placate the Donbass Diesel Monster and manoeuvred past the myopic yellow Fiat 500. The driver gave me one of those, "I'm going straight to HR" looks. Living his life in the same manner as his driving, I am sure.

Late evening, we arrived in Warsaw. Weaving through the traffic I just followed our lead vehicle (in that maintaining the integrity of the convoy trumps the highway code type way). I made many friends, sailing across roundabouts and threatening to exchange my rust with a $250,000 Mercedes that decided that it wanted to cut in front of me. All is fair in love, war and most especially Warsaw commuter traffic.

On arrival at our accommodation, we went straight for a meal and then to bed. Tomorrow was going to be a very long day.

DAY 2

BREAKFAST WAS THE usual is-anyone-else-even-alive level of early. Having seen the itinerary for the day, I quietly stuffed myself. The likelihood of a decent meal in the next 18 hours would be slim to none. Back on the road, I was joined by a new member of the team, Krystian. Igor suggested Krystian drive as he thought I drove too slowly! I drive in the English style, I protested. That is to say, in a manner that acknowledges other road users (not common practice in Eastern Europe). Poor Krystian seemed rather embarrassed as I shuffled over to the passenger side. I was secretly quite happy as the passenger seat was infinitely more comfortable than the driver's. Cleaner too.

JULY CONVOY

The heat of the day was already building. Despite the open windows, the temperature in the Donbas Diesel was alarming. Krystian optimistically opened the side vents only to be blasted by a shower of dust and oven-ready air. We both laughed. He was just that bit too young to remember long hot 1970s car journeys where no AC was the norm, replete with those cheap plastic seats that burned your legs. It all felt very retro to me.

My mind wandered back to a certain 1976 car journey. It was a top five falling out with Dad moment. Aged six and very into my Crayola crayons (still the best medium for handwriting in my opinion) I left my complete set in the back window of Dad's brand-new Morris Marina. After a whole scorching afternoon at the beach, we returned (as a happy family) to discover a rainbow puddle of wax integrated with the synthetic material that made up the back shelf and back seat. Both Dad and I were very upset. I thought Dad shared my grief at the loss of a world-beating set of crayons. He seemed more concerned about the freakish damage I had done to his car. To this day I am pretty sure that a full set of Crayola crayons is worth more than a Morris Marina.

Chatting with Krystian, I discovered that he had not had the best start in life, but through dedication and hard graft had managed to build up a couple of businesses and really turn things around. He now felt it was time to lend help where it was really needed. This was his first run into Ukraine. We talked a bit about our wives and how they felt about us going. We agreed that staying at home and waiting for news was and always will be a very tough ask. Regular updates as often as possible was my main advice. I could see that Krystian was a man of practical common sense, honest with himself and others. He would be a huge asset in Ukraine over the coming days in terms of morale and just doing the right thing.

With the combination of chatting and 80s music, the

border was suddenly looming. Igor was on the comms arranging our final RV before we crossed.

We pulled into the car park of Biedronka, the last shop in Poland. A totemic place that on past trips heralded either our arrival or departure from Ukraine. They also do a rather nice line in banana milk too, the ultimate comfort food in my opinion.

There we were met by the legendary Polish NBA player, Marcin Gortat. Marcin is probably one of the best-known sports figures in Poland and has been a huge supporter of Ukraine and Igor's convoys. From the moment his beaming enormous frame emerged from his equally enormous vehicle, everyone around us was taking photographs and pointing. It was quite a moment! While poor Marcin was being inundated with selfie requests and strangers irrationally sprinting towards him across the car park, Anatoliy beckoned me over to the Donbas Diesel Monster. I could tell that he cared little for celebrity and more about how best to guide the nightmare diesel creature across the border. It needed someone of Anatoliy's heft and charm to work with both sets of border guards to facilitate a crossing. The beast displayed an ancient Scandinavian registration plate. I also suspected it had been devoid of official paperwork for much of the last decade. A borderline barn find, at the border!

Forming up into our convoy running order, we trundled out of the supermarket car park, past endless vehicles with doors flung open, passengers and drivers alike seeking refuge on this terribly hot day. As we gathered speed, both roadsides revealed people sleeping under the remotest excuse for shade - the best dressed homeless people I had ever seen.

One man in a preppie style beige suit lay in the foetal position on a patch of dirt, shaded under a bush that had pretensions of being a tree. In normal circumstances one might pass him off as a drunk. Under the current circumstances this was an exhausted man with an uncertain future. In the sucking flash of vehicle after vehicle, similar momentarily surreal tableaus emerged and disappeared. Varying stories of fear and desperation revealed themselves, hidden between vehicles, shelters and vans along this vast stretch of road. A doddery old man grappling with his stick. A mother changing her new-born baby's nappy. A bus driver struggling with an overfilled luggage compartment. An old lady staring blankly into the abyss. We would never know the conclusions to these stories - a myriad of unsolved human suffering micro-mysteries. All this in the dry stifling heat.

Looking down that long straight road to the border, perspective shrinking the crossing point to little green blocks, I tell myself that we are not queue-jumping. Looking at the faces of those we pass, I know in their eyes we are just arrogant charity people, all V8 engines and no idea. I know that is how I would feel. However, we had a schedule to keep and people waiting for us. One must develop a strange mixture of hardness and compassion in this line of work.

We were waved straight through to the border checks. Again, Anatoliy and Igor are past masters at this. Watching the body language and expressions of all concerned, there are unfathomable politics and pantomimes at play which I am not equipped for. I realise that as much as we have in common, there are cultural aspects to hierarchies and dialogue that move beyond linguistic issues. Observing such moments makes me realise what excellent leaders Anatoliy and Igor are. If it was me trying to traverse the border we would still be there!

Another observation I made was the contrast in the weather. I found myself standing in the exact spot at the border, where the previous December I remember thinking, this is the coldest I had ever been. Now in the blistering heat

I was almost the hottest I had ever been. Central and Eastern European weather is very unforgiving. Not exactly a ground-breaking revelation, I grant you, but one that strangely informs those other cultural differences I was talking about. Hard conditions breed hard people.

Back on the road the border post behind us, we were on the secure comms liaising with our first drop. Anatoliy was in his element behind the wheel of the Donbas Diesel Monster. He gave me a wicked grin as we growled out onto the main road in a fog of dust and heat haze. The countryside looked beautiful. I was amazed at the proliferation of wild-flowers and insects, many of whom decided to join us through the open windows. Sucked in by the vortex created by the speeding beast, I was wrestling with some form of supersized horse fly, when the radio bleeped into life.

"Slow down, slow down."

Anatoliy grinned at me and made a vague attempt to reduce his speed for about ten seconds.

The Diesel Monster had a mind of its own and we were off again past orchards and babushkas replete with headscarves and hand scythes, working in the way I imagined countless babushkas had done forever. The scenes of bucolic charm and simple life could lull one into a false sense of cliché. Look! The perfect life I was telling myself, living off the land. An honest life. Decent values. The image was then dashed as we flashed passed two leggy supermodels in hot pants, arguing and waving bejewelled mobile phones at each other outside a luxury car dealership. Would they ever end up as babushkas in headscarves with scythes, I wondered? Scythes would be a bad idea at this juncture, as indeed hot pants would be for those babushkas.

The convoy was catching up with us now and we were reaching our first drop point. We passed a cemetery that had become a familiar landmark on our supply route. Sadly,

the cemetery was less familiar now due to its expansion.
Fresh graves marked by unit flags, national flags and flowers.
Mothers staring in silent pain at crosses and pictures of
previously healthy sons and daughters. Wobbly lip time. A
terrible price is being paid. I caught Anatoliy's eye and nothing
needed to be said.

The rendezvous was made in a well-remembered lane that
we have come to know and love over the months. In the winter
it was a terrifying frozen slide of a track, lashed by an icy wind.
Last December my feet skated along the road surface, tarmac
preserved below an impenetrable layer of ice. Only manual
work maintained a survivable body temperature. Now the track
was a baked biscuit of a road.

The contrast of winter and summer in Ukraine is
bewildering. A fine cement grade dust coated everything
it touched, particularly sweaty middle-aged men! I had a
moment to stretch before the rest of the convoy rounded
the bend and Igor was on the ground determining the order
of unloading. A battered van appeared. Out jumped our
December friends from the university! Big hugs and quick
catch-ups were silenced by Igor who demanded a quick
turnaround. We had to cover another 500km that day. Despite
the banter and joshing we were in a war zone. There was a
schedule. Some of the equipment we were delivering was time
sensitive. Igor was also carrying another huge responsibility -
our safety and welfare.

The afternoon heat appeared to build with each gust
of wind. No cool breezes here. Quite the reverse. We began
shifting our delivery of heavy unforgiving boxes by hand,
each one a surprising weight, always exceeding perceived
expectations. The excited chatter very rapidly settled into a
puffing silence. Gurning faces passed me as I returned to our
trailers to be loaded up with gear again. The university van

rapidly filled up. Goodness knows what the tonnage limit was. The engineers at Peugeot would certainly be chuffed with our stress-testing efforts!

Load completed, our academic friends hugged us and quickly departed. I noted how physically tough they had become since our first meeting seven months before. Medieval historians were now he-men. Literature professors shifted fifteen kilo boxes like seasoned navvies. There was a terrible focus to their work too. I sadly suspected that they no longer really cared much about which Teutonic Knight had dominated the region in the middle-ages or the merits of investigating the unusual pentameter of an obscure 19th century poem. They just cared about their students fighting and dying in the Donbas and Kherson. It was both sad and inspiring to see the change in them.

With the university van bouncing and creaking into the distance, the Donbas Diesel Monster was handed over to its new owners. As I removed my kit from the monster, I contemplated its fate. Someone told me front line vehicles lasted about a month. A month? Apparently (I discovered with strange relief) the trucks often fall to bits before they are destroyed. They are driven with such abandon, in the mad maze of tracks and country lanes that make up the front, mechanical failure often does for them before the Russians do. The good news is that the vehicles go on to donate vital parts to keep other vehicles on the road. A form of motorised donor scheme. For some reason that made me feel better about saying goodbye to the Donbas Diesel Monster.

Back in the vehicles, I was driving with Krystian again. The first thing I noticed was the blessed AC. After two days of blasting heat it felt like Nirvana. For five minutes. I held out for as long as I could. Shivering, I asked him to turn it down as I looked for a long sleeve top.

JULY CONVOY

The Ukrainian countryside looked beautiful in the early evening sun. Families were sitting in their gardens, some deep in discussion, others pointing out flowers or choosing which piece of meat they wanted from a deliciously smoking BBQ. An old lady walked her skipping little dog. Only the sight of a soldier pausing momentarily at his gatepost to contemplate the emotional barrier between the front and leave indicated that there was a war on. A golden onion domed church shone in the distance. In that moment it was as though we were on a lovely summer drive. Bleep. Our comms chattered into life. We were stopping for food.

Opening the truck door delivered another regrettable air conditioning moment. The false comfort of artificial cool air versus the oven door burning of evening heat. A few short steps to the café and it was back to next level cooling air conditioning. Again, it was hard to imagine we were in war zone. The brand-new café was very stylishly appointed and very well designed. As Igor briefed us regarding the next 24 hours I could not help thinking that this is possibly the hippest roadside café I had ever been in. Great service, beautiful salads and food.

As we hit the road a summer storm was brewing. The evening darkened and flashes silhouetted the gently rolling hills.

"I'm sure that's lightning," I said. "Then again it might not be."

The sudden heavy lashing rain indicated that it was a natural storm and not a Russian one! For hundreds of kilometres, we passed through contrasting beautiful sunsets and dark carwashes of rain. Krystian and I traded our life stories and tried to explain what had brought us to Ukraine. In conclusion, he turned to me and simply stated, "If not us, then who?" I could not have said it better.

THE WAR NEXT DOOR

After eighteen hours of being on the go there is a point where exhaustion can become dangerous. The comms had been silent for almost an hour. Then bleep. That blessed bleep, followed by Anatoliy's voice indicating our accommodation was only 25 km away! Yes! 25 km in Ukraine feels like just around the corner! Morale lifted again, Krystian and I talked about the virtues of our respective sleeping mats, sleeping bags and just how quickly we were going to fall asleep. It was not to be.

In the distance we could see a large white building. On leaving the road we pulled onto a drive worthy of any stately home and meandered towards a construction that was clearly taking the form of a luxury hotel. Surely, we could not be staying here? What about my lovely sleeping bag? I want my hard floor and insects!

The jokes stopped abruptly as Krystian killed the engine. The only sound was an air raid siren. The distinctive wail rapidly stripped us of the ersatz cloak of safety provided by the truck cabin. Doors open, the volume of the siren increased. The heat of the night compounded by the lack of air con added to a strange new tension. Only the clumsy insects seemed oblivious to the siren, bouncing off chiaroscuro faces and back into the night.

We were met by the hotel's relaxed yet professionally concerned security staff who guided us through quiet gardens and manicured lawns. The juxtaposition of luxury and war seemed almost dreamlike in my exhausted state. The bizarre did not stop there. Presented with our room cards we were asked, had we eaten recently? The receptionist received a range of weary "Noes." It was the sort of involuntary collective groan that school children make when a previous disappointment might stand a chance of being rectified. We could only hope.

I went straight to my room to be confronted with what

can only be described as special anniversary weekend grade luxury. A basket in the bathroom displayed bottles of expensive lotions and gels. There was a beautiful marble "watering can" shower. A robe and pile of fluffy white towels sat next to slippers embroidered with the hotel logo. 48 hours previously my wife had watched me pack my Bergen. I recalled earnestly telling her, I will be living out of this for a week. I felt a fraud. Only the siren outside sounding the "all clear" allowed me to reclaim some roughing-it credibility.

It got worse! The room phone rang. It was Anatoliy. "Come and eat, my room."

As I crept along the corridor to his room, I was joined by other team members. Before us lay what must be described as a fine dining taster picnic. At a quarter past one in the morning! I was allegedly in a war zone, the very last thing in the world I was expecting was to be eating fois gras sliders garnished with a savoury mushroom jam at 1.15am, having just finished an air raid.

We were all a bit stunned. This was clearly the hotel's idea of a midnight feast. What would my lovely wife say if she could see me now? I know that sympathy levels would be at an all-time low. All of us were wondering how best to explain the situation to our better halves. Filled with fois gras at 1.30am, I went to sleep. I sent a simple message to Jula saying we were OK. I refrained from saying so was the savoury mushroom jam. That wasn't OK. That was just plain delicious!

DAY 3

AT LEAST THE early start compensated for the luxurious surroundings we found ourselves in. The breakfast was in keeping with the fois gras snack of a few hours before. Exceptional and delicious. Looking around I could see that we really were the only guests. Haunted by happier times, I imagined the place teeming with wedding parties or couples on a sumptuous weekend break. This morning's scene however was of a quiet, less demonstrative Ukrainian sadness. The veneer of luxury could not hide the economic damage the war was doing to this rather lovely hotel. The staff were delightful, but with no guests, the service was almost personal. I had my own breakfast butler. On checking out I vowed to bring my wife back here one day.

An hour later we were seated in a factory collecting a Polish-American journalist, Mania, and her cameraman, Yaro. They had come from a particularly grim part of the frontline and were enjoying a bit of respite in the factory café. If only they knew where we had just come from! On hearing me speak English, she began interviewing me straight away. I cannot remember what I said but hopefully it was not too mad. I can be a little Cromwellian in the morning.

Departing the factory, we were now most definitely heading east and into a powerful morning sun. Yaro sat with me in the back of the truck. We conversed in a mix of Polish and Google translate. Aged 21, he had been finishing up film school in Kyiv. The plan was to graduate and make movies. Then February 24th 2022 happened. The young graduate found himself reflexively documenting the horror unfolding before his disbelieving eyes.

Along with Mania, he had been one of the first to witness and document the massacres around Bucha and Irpin. Following that baptism of fire, his combination of technical skill, local knowledge and daring (he was a free fall parachutist in his spare time) found him quickly in demand as a camera for hire. It was not a job he wanted. He wanted his family back. He wanted his life back. Only his brother remained in Ukraine.

We chatted about Poland and the UK – both places he

hoped to see. When he said "hoped" it was clear that he had to balance his hopes with the reality of the dangers in Ukraine. Observing him, one moment he was the 21-year-old kid juggling the latest media tech, the next, he was talking with a wisdom beyond his years. Lost years. 21-year-olds should not be finding mass graves forty-five minutes' walk from the family home. No one should.

We changed the subject and discussed why my Polish was so awful after seven years of living in Poland. My excuse was that I work in English and my wife speaks English. After a lengthy debate about linguistics, we decided that I was old and old people always struggle with languages. I felt so much better!

As we relaxed into the journey, I thought how extraordinary a day in Ukraine can become. Here we were, a Polish businessman, Ukrainian film student, a New York Pole and a middle-aged Brit all heading into the Donbas. I have come to think that an hour spent with anyone under these conditions is equal to a year of friendship under normal circumstances. Outside, the endless clear blue sky and golden crops (mirroring the flag of Ukraine as the design intended) stretched out before us on a scale and perspective that this little islander struggled to fathom.

We passed through pretty little villages, the kind with one local business that was clearly the main employer. The quality of the roads was surprisingly good. Only occasionally did we have to slow down, usually for an inexplicable stretch of twenty metre dirt track that broke up the finely metalled road. Sometimes at these dirt track breaks, local people would come running forward and hand us delicious homemade cakes and very welcome chilled homemade juices, known as "kompot". This was their very public way of supporting people headed to the front. These people had little but what they did have they were giving with love to those who were headed into harm's way. They were kind, decent people who had already suffered a great deal. The many fluttering flags in the little village cemeteries were testament to that. Wobbly lip time.

We were headed for a city that is a focal point for transport to the east and for those coming back from the front. My last visit to the city had been in early spring. Back then the streets appeared dark and grim. In the brilliant sunlight of July the place felt warm and inviting, more like an industrial Mediterranean city. The strong light bathed buildings in a glow that seemed to bleach the harsh edges off the Soviet era blocks. The centre of the city was a mix of lovely restaurants, al fresco dining and again I was reminded of a workaday Nice or Florence. Despite the fact that the place had sustained much damage during the war, to my eyes the people seemed busy and relaxed. I felt that mid-afternoon vibe that you would find in any functioning urban environment. Only the concrete hoop shelters on the streets (designed for the public caught out and about in an air raid) suggested that air of normality could be erased in a second.

Arriving at our destination we were met by a young couple who were the driving force behind raising funding and requests across Europe for the main hospital's medical supplies. They seemed far too young to be so well organised. The way they engaged with us, other volunteers and medical staff impressed me so much I had to be reminded we had some unloading to do! War has an extraordinary ability to empower those who can do. Gone are the usual rhythms of time served and aged-based seniority. If you can do the job, you get the job. 21-year-old maths teachers can suddenly find themselves commanding 120 people in an intelligence unit. They have the skills, so give them the job. You find this all over Ukraine now. I hate to say it, but war creates the most efficient form of meritocracy!

Once unloading was completed, the couple wanted to organise a photo for social media. Everyone is very media savvy in Ukraine. The power of the media has been instrumental in maintaining support, and the supply of everything from MRI scanners to homemade balaclavas. A medical team was brought out to pose with us. Despite their visible fatigue and 20 hour working-day stress they very cheerfully obliged, knowing that the social media momentum would keep their work supported. Photo taken, they disappeared immediately to begin a scheduled amputation.

Some of the equipment we delivered would also be needed for that amputation and the subsequent amputations that would take the team into the early hours of the morning. I watched the medics and our deliveries disappear into the temporary facility and wondered what horrific sights lay behind the old wooden doors.

Another couple walked past, approximately my age. He was wearing a blue blazer and a Panama hat. She was wearing a very English frock and wide brimmed hat. They could have been going straight to Wimbledon or Henley. In all my years I cannot recall a more incongruous sight. What was their story? They must have been going somewhere, a wedding, the local regatta? Bizarre!! No one else seemed to see them. They walked and moved in a very English way too. Could they have been on holiday?? My brain had gone from contemplating traumatic amputations to trying to identify the ribbon of the gentleman's Panama hat in about five seconds. Was that Harrow or an Oxford college?

The young couple who were organising the donations suddenly appeared before me.

"Where are you from in the UK?"

"Where are THEY from in the UK?" I wanted to ask about the older frock and Panama hat wearing couple who had now disappeared.

"I've lived most of my adult life in London but have actually lived in Poland for the past seven years."

We had a lovely chat about finding more support for Ukraine and how impressed I was with what they were doing. What was equally impressive was their flawless English to the point that their accent was almost English. More mysteries and no time to ask questions. We had to go. We had miles to go.

We crossed the great river which really feels like a barrier between the war zone and the relatively peaceful parts of Ukraine. This feeling is of course illusory. All of Ukraine was being regularly targeted by Russian missiles. Indeed, I remember telling Oksana (who had joined our convoy in Poland needing a lift to a city in the north) that at least she would be safer there rather than in the Donbas. That night missiles rained down on her district landing only a couple of hundred metres from where she was staying. Nowhere in Ukraine was really that safe. However, from a geographical perspective, in the physical act of crossing that great river there is a sense of foreboding commitment. On reaching the other side there are no natural barriers between you and the war. Now only the heroic Ukrainian army stood between you, the Russian invader and the terrible violence of the front.

With the physical protection of the river behind us, a new mood settled over our vehicle. Soon we would be entering the military zone where the comforting multinational logos of commerce and familiar branding of fast food would be gone. The pan-European civilian world of families and normal daily life would give way to the quieter roads of war.

Reaching into my Sainsbury's sandwich bag (the cause of much mirth), I found a mysterious package. Strands of something wrapped in silver. Carefully I pulled back the foil to discover a wadge of liquorice "Flyers" that my darling wife had hidden away. She must have known what a morale boost they would be and how much discovering them would mean to me. What a wonderful woman. It was most definitely big wobbly lip, staring out of the window with shades on - blinky tears time!

With great and secret ceremony, I began munching on a liquorice Flyer, that most British of confections. Surely, I must be the first person to bring liquorice Flyers into the Ukrainian military zone?

The aniseed flavours unleashed strange feelings of summers past and the scary passage of time compressed into that instant. The flavours of childhood, holidays and memories of a den in my grandparents' garden combined to comfort me. I never thought I would be eating my favourite liquorice sweets in a war zone, so far from home. Then again, maybe I was just overthinking the situation.

Wishing to break my selfish secrecy, I offered the Flyers to my fellow passengers. I fully expected them to join me in my nostalgia. It was not to be. The liquorice epiphany failed almost immediately. Mania chewed and then spat New York style complete with New York style language. Yaro politely nibbled and gently nodded with the face of a diplomat. I could read his mind though. "Brits actually eat this crap?" Only Krystian said something vaguely complementary about the UK having the best sweets. In the end the only people I found in the whole of Ukraine who liked the Flyers were people living right on the frontline. They had endured the Russian occupation, months of fighting and suffering. In retrospect I have also come to believe that they too were only being polite.

The traffic was thinning out now. I remembered this phenomenon from last time. After half an hour the civilian world had largely evaporated. The highway's sole purpose now was to feed the war. No civilian (save for the odd dutiful farmer using the main drag to move a combine or tractor to another field) was to be seen on the road. There were families that had chosen to stay but it was also clear many had decided to head west. We pretty much had the road to ourselves.

The quiet of the evening only broken by the terrifying dinosaur engine roar of the occasional pod of ageing ZIL trucks, joined in song by their primordial tyres moaning along the highway. Drivers peering over giant, ancient steering wheels, worn to a brilliant sheen by years of fearful sweaty hands. Or the occasional mini-bus full of soldiers, some sleeping, playing cards or laughing.

On registering we were foreign aid volunteers, the body of the bus would rock with great waves of enthusiastic soldiers clambering over seats, crushing slumbering colleagues against windows, all smiley shouts and gang signs, a spontaneous demonstration of fraternal love. A solidarity and respect earned through the shared fear and pride of heading in the same dangerous direction. These moments were both hilarious and inspiring. Some of their faces remain seared into my memory. A funny hat or distinctive beard. Exceptionally young faces. I wonder what they are doing now or if they are even still alive?

The convoy was coming to a halt on a particularly dry and dusty patch of land. Igor was out and indicating that Krystian and I should retrieve a very heavy box from one of compartments on his truck. My goodness, that thing weighed a ton. As we manhandled the great trunk to the front of the vehicle, the familiarity of the location caught up with me. This was none other than the legendary volunteer-run dining café we last visited a few months back. The mud and filth of April had been converted (by the gas mark 10 Ukrainian summer) into the sort of dust bowl Steinbeck would have been proud of. Out came the friendly babushkas who fell upon the trunk, thrilled with its contents of tuna, tinned goods, bread and other delights. This was our contribution to the collective, and the tanned and grinning babushkas beckoned us into their lovingly crafted food den.

Krystian and I were last into the shed. Just before entering a young Ukrainian soldier held out an arm and thanked us for coming, for being foreign witnesses to what was happening. We tried to shake his hand, but it soon became clear that he was badly wounded. Great red welts and some form of orthopaedic pins worked their way around the top of his arm. He was on light duties and driving "white fleet" around the rear areas. In most western armies he would still be in a hospital. We wished him luck and left him hobbling and grimacing back to his vehicle. He turned and gave me a massive grin and a victory sign. If only I had a camera.

Back in April the heat of the medieval stoves had been an overwhelming memory on entering the dining shed. Now, the outside temperature was so fierce that I did not even notice the difference - the stoves may have been cooler than the outside! The only constant from April were the bright red, beaming faces of the hardy babushkas, stirring vast cauldrons of borsht and tasty stews, nodding and smiling with love at the passing soldiers. A little reminder of home to those who may never see home again.

In the dining shed, a great contraption pumped cool air providing welcome respite to those who had been baking in the trenches. Tanned warriors greeted us with hearty "Good evenings." Igor and Anatoliy were quizzed by the curious. Our clothing was a confusing mix of outdoor wear and military wear – who were we? Igor and Anatoliy fielded many questions. Krystian, Yaro and I focussed on eating. Yaro looked on horrified as I resurrected my Donbas field sandwich recipe. Bread and raw onion. Am I the only one?

We continued into the east. The magic hour of light now

upon us. Yaro was filming and wanted to record my thoughts on the Donbas. In the golden evening glow, I told the camera that the Donbas was just beautiful. Indeed, it was. The countryside resembled the summer parched fields of Tuscany or southern France. The terracotta colours and rolling shadows were reminiscent of balmy warm holiday evenings, the sort that improvised BBQs and funny local beers are made for. It was possible to delude oneself quite successfully.

Except we were now under military escort. Obvious routes were not being taken. The comms would bleep and new information would send us under the cover of drone proof trees or a smashed up bus stop. Military vehicles would thunder past at speeds which told you that however charming the countryside appeared to be, nothing was normal here. At one point a group of soldiers in just their underpants dashed across the road like a herd of wildebeest. We began singing songs to boost morale. In the bubble of our truck cabin, we laughed out loud at the incongruity of it all. It turned out Krystian had rather a good voice. Think a Polish Ed Sheeran.

We stopped again. The sun had dropped below the hills now. The escort reminded us that we can only wee on the tarmac. It was too dangerous now to step off the highway. I checked the wind direction and did as I was told. We all felt sorry for Mania and faced the other way. Mania had been in Ukraine for some time. I think with what she had seen she was past embarrassment. If anything, it was the rest of us who were embarrassed!

Darkness was nearly upon us. Before we headed back to the vehicles our escorts became very serious. One instinctively knew it was time to shut up. Soon we would be very very close to the front. We were told to lower our voices. No torches. Stay undercover. Be drone aware. Once at the location do as you are told when you are told. Only move under escort.

On arrival at our accommodation the vehicles went straight under cover. We stayed put until taken by a military unit member (again under cover) into our accommodation. We were shown a bed space, our kit was left in the room and then we were escorted to a dining area. All this in near enough silence and total darkness. The path to the dining area involved crossing an open patch of land and the feeling of exposure was childishly exhilarating. Moving in irregular groups we bounded towards the canteen building, guessing where best to place our feet.

As my lanky legs knocked and twisted over the uneven ground, I imagined a Russian drone locking onto me. Childish nerves had me chuckling to myself in a completely inappropriate way. Hopefully no one heard or saw me. Sometimes my nervous reaction to frightening situations is laughter. I know in the past this has led some people into thinking I am quite mad, which is of course entirely possible.

The dining area was an eclectic mix of surviving furniture, Heath Robinson chairs and a row of theatre seats. Yaro, Mania and I took C12, 13 and 14 respectively. Igor, Anatoliy and Krystian placed themselves on a bench made in haste from nails, pallets and a plank of old wood. Insects also piled into the room. The heat of the day was trapped into this memory of a dining space. It was a magnet for every six-legged flying creature in the area. Our military escorts joined us along with seniors from our host unit. The dim light revealed some rather tasty meat and salad dishes.

Crump, CRUMP!

"Normally they are done for the day," said Mania checking her watch. "Actually it's later than I thought so now I'm not surprised." In this sector, apparently, the bad guys like to fire a few artillery rounds around midnight just to keep people on their toes. A Russian lullaby.

I looked around the table. You could tell that this unit was exhausted. They sat hunched, uncomfortably crumpled in the heat, the ingrained, operational grubbiness sweating through their deep tans, war stress behind the eyes. They stared, reacting not thinking, living with artillery, drones, constant danger. They masked their fatigue with funny stories and the impeccable manners of those who are on their best behaviour for visitors. Weary, gracious hosts. These guys needed some leave.

Someone disappeared, returning quickly with a flimsy plastic bottle and a hand full of coke cans. Shot glasses were produced and distributed whether you wanted one or not. For our group I suspected not. For our host unit though, I suspect that the clear liquid in the flimsy plastic bottle was a brief escape from the madness of their environment. Shots were poured. A toast was made. Shots were downed. Glasses were then refilled with magical speed.

Over the years I had learned that in the Slavic world communal drinking and specifically communal shot drinking can be a political minefield (if you pardon the pun). I have also learned from previous experience that if you are not driving the next day then you must be a designated drinker. I looked around the table. The first shot was still burning its way through everyone's body. This was no shop-bought vodka. The collapsing plastic bottle contained a dreadful homebrew, the toxicity challenging the very integrity of the container itself. Moonshine hydro-carbons.

Anatoliy looked around and rose to his feet proposing a toast to our host unit, to victory and to Ukraine. At that moment two flies landed in my shot glass. They died instantly. I swear that on contact with the liquid there was a psst noise, like a hot match plunging into water. I desperately tried to fish out the flies, but they were rapidly dissolving in the poison. Everyone was on their feet now. Drink, drink!! I thought of where we were and what those flies might have been feasting on. Drink, Drink! I tossed the drink into my mouth. Instant fire. Flies forgotten. No amount of cola could dilute that feeling of unregulated alcohol hitting the stomach. The shot glass was filled again before I had even sat down. Another crump echoed in the distance.

Igor stood up and said after a very long day we needed to get some sleep. Maybe it was the artillery round that indicated to Igor that we needed to get back to the accommodation. However, I suspect Igor was saving Anatoliy and myself from being drawn into a drinking vortex that would make us quite useless the next day. We had satisfied the etiquette of drinking with our hosts. There was no need to wreck the next day in the process.

Back across the open ground. The fear of the drones and exposure to the sky had us moving with primitive focus. Once more under cover we found our sleeping area. The windows had been blacked out. We were now allowed a dim light to prepare sleeping bags. The lamps provided an unnatural candlelight effect, shadows and illumination in all the wrong places, revealing the room's original purpose. The drawings and pictures on the wall indicated that the space was once a classroom. I had the strangest feeling in that room. Despite everything it felt like a happy place. Or at least the ghost of happiness lived there.

Half a photo of a joyful school event lay torn and hanging from a solitary pin on the wall. Hooks with cartoon animal stickers indicated where little Dima or Oksana should hang their coats. There were sweet little spaces for sweet little shoes under each peg. We all looked around the room, peering like archaeologists at the evidence, piecing together the magnitude of the war. The tragedy of these lives, rediscovering a lost world through these children's drawings and crushed projects. A lost world. In stark contrast there were grid square diagrams relating to directing effective mortar fire onto enemy positions filling the blackboard at the end of the room. Still being used as a classroom we concurred.

The school caretaker appeared to make sure we were happy and comfortable. He seemed very pleased to see us. He stood rubbing his hands like an overly keen B&B host. He showed me to the washroom and apologised. I explained in my halting Polish that I didn't mind about the damage. His eyes welled up and he gripped my hand in thanks leaving me to clean my teeth. There was running water but no one in their right might would use it. You would have been better off using the unit's homebrew vodka. Safer even. Instead, I opted for my travel mouthwash, which thanks to my consumption of that lethal homebrew had lost any of its normal kick. Indeed, now it did taste like water!

Back in the corridor the caretaker emerged out of the gloom and engaged me in conversation. Through my weak Polish and half understanding, it was clear that he loved his school. He regaled me with happy memories of the community and the children. The conversational gear then changed. His eyes hardened as he relayed the chaos and descent into madness that had seen the school metamorphosize into a nightmare front line location.

I tried to tell him what a good job he was doing in keeping the school going ready for the children to come back. My bad Polish just had him nodding politely.

"Children, yes, children," he said in Ukrainian. Children is the same word in Polish too. I really wanted to comfort him but was limited by language and not wanting to make a proud man cry. He hugged me and disappeared down another corridor into the darkness. A Miss Havisham like figure, the sense of loss palpable. Sadness and nostalgia surrounding him.

Once in the dormitory room, I could feel the booze kicking in. We were lucky enough to be provided with sun lounger type beds. I lay there and was rather grateful that I had not left my three litre "Camelback" water bottle in the vehicle. Mania and Yaro giggled as I wolfed about half a litre in one gulp. The others encouraged me to drink some more.

"I'm not that bad," I protested.

Or was I? All dorms act as an accelerant when it comes to teasing and general leg-pulling. Everyone locked onto my drinking bottle.

"What's in there?"

"You are out of control."

Bigger laughs rang out as Anatoliy entered the room and acted as though my water-drinking meant I was at it again. We all began to relax. As the volume of chatter slowly increased the outside world ceased to exist. We had forgotten where we were as stories were told and anecdotes tested.

Krystian strode into the room, probably like the old form teacher of this very classroom had done on many occasions.

"I can hear you down the corridor."

His body language was more powerful than his words. Nothing more needed to be said. We shrank back to gentle talking, grateful for the admonishment with respect to our safety. As common sense returned, we carefully packed our kit, making sure we were ready to move at a moment's notice should we be attacked. We were maybe six kilometres from the front line.

Here we were bedding down in a wrecked building. What a contrast to the previous night's five-star accommodation. The newly silent room was soon ready for bed. Lights out. In the heat and darkness of the Donbas night I suppressed thoughts of artillery, the potential for sudden fire and flying concrete. More crumps sounded through the walls, I prayed they would stay in the distance. We all slept clothed. Here if you have to move you must be ready to move. Surviving trumps comfortable sleeping.

DAY 4

ONLY A FEW hours sleep were possible amid the institutionalised cacophony of a dormitory at night. How many snorers in our group, I wondered? Later I discovered I am about mid-table in the snoring league, so just as well I keep my thoughts to myself. Packed in an instant, we waited for our minders to escort us to the vehicles. It was daylight now and prime drone time.

We sat silently in the room. Yaro and Anatoliy politely giggled as I mimicked drinking from the Camelback. Thankfully I felt OK. The half-expected hangover did not materialise. Adrenaline plus water cures all, it seems. Footsteps in the corridor activated a new sense of urgency. Patient waiting became anxious movement with a command to "Follow me."

Under cover we reached our vehicles and began loading our kit. I caught the eye of a couple of soldiers under tree cover across the way.   They gave me a stress-ridden, stay-where-you-are smile, no wave. Outdoor movement is a give-away. We were also joined by Sacha who would act as one of our military minders. It was lovely to see him again. He looked a little meaner and leaner but that was only to be expected after the last few months.

Comms were quietly checked, and a final brief was given. I only understood about a quarter of it, but enough to know that today was going to be tough. There was no talk of breakfast. I just hoped the drones could not detect rumbling tummies. Mine threatened to out-rumble the artillery in the distance.

Our vehicles roared out of the gate, the quicker we moved the less of a target we were. Being first out of the gate brought back memories of Iraq, the same morning heat building and the sense that you were being watched. In Basra the threat of being the first on the ground always begged the question, what had the insurgent bombers managed to plant overnight? First out of the gate meant being the first to find out. Now the threat came from the air in the form of drones. Same dread from a different direction.

We joined an MSR for about an hour and then began twisting and turning our way through suburbia. The city limits gave way to pleasant streets. A warm morning sun gave the place a genuinely welcoming feel. We pulled into a rather impressive public square. I was about to point out a grand columned building to Yaro when I shut my mouth in shock. The street before us was smashed and ripped apart.

We stopped the vehicles and jumped out. Shop fronts were crushed right back into their back storerooms. Rubble and glass strewn everywhere. Turning a corner, a bar/café lay eviscerated. We tentatively ventured into the café, numbed by the sudden magnitude of the damage and the unearthly silence. How could so much destruction be so silent? The scene was so violent it almost needed noise to make it more palatable, less horrific. The quiet created a suffocatingly inescapable vacuum of nightmarish reality.

I looked at the bar. Drinks lay waiting to be collected. A till receipt fluttered in a handheld card reader, halfway through its last transaction, capturing the moment of oblivion. A glass of cola sat on its table, ignorant of the horror and terrible forces unleashed around it. How had those cups and drink remained intact? The adrenalised mind will focus on such absurdities when overloaded with visceral catastrophe.

Already Yaro and Mania were moving and filming,

respectfully capturing what the world does not see. There was a twisting almost balletic rhythm to how those two moved through the devastation. Then the smell hits you. It came with a waft of morning heat. Yaro turned towards me. We locked eyes. Nothing needed to be said. I learned that smell in Iraq. Yaro learned it in Bucha. It catches you out with its pungent proximity. You now step with even more care. Not everyone or everything had been retrieved yet by the emergency services.

The Russian missile had struck a happy buzzing bar and shopping centre. It was a place where younger people gathered and hung out. A place where you might take a first girlfriend for a meal, a place where a quiet coffee and biscotti might just make the war feel that little bit further away than it really was. Until it was not. Many people had died and many more were injured.

A makeshift shrine had been set up outside. We paid our respects and got back in the vehicles.

"Bastards, bastards, bastards!" I hissed in an almost silly, inadequate outburst. Anatoliy and Sacha yelled worse in Ukrainian. The level of anger was such that we had to get a grip of ourselves and focus. Create a new file in the brain and quickly move the last twenty minutes into it. We had aid that needed delivering to people who needed us.

The route out of the city led us through the focus of recent fighting. Knocked-out tanks and armoured vehicles indicated the titanic battles that had taken place along this earlier front. There were signs of massive destruction on either side of the route. Trees appeared to be neatly cropped for hundreds of metres at a time. The arboreal scything of artillery was responsible for these surreal gaps in the flora.

At first the smashed houses and villages were shocking in their freakish variety. Nothing had survived intact. But the "nothing" was always different. Half a house with a full roof. A whole house with no roof. Garage doors blown into squashed rectangles reinstalled into the road. Street after street. Hamlet after hamlet - for a solid two hours of driving. The true extent of this wasteland is hard to comprehend. We have not seen damage meeting the horizon like this since World War 2. Imagine a two-hour drive at 100km an hour through Oradour-Sur-Glane. Endless to the point of apocalyptic.

We stopped for breakfast at a little village. The heat of the day was now stifling. The scene was one of constant movement. Cafés and burger bars fed those on route to the front, from the front and anywhere in between. Igor suggested we grab a late breakfast. Breakfast? Standing in the stinking rubble of that restaurant had made me forget about breakfast completely. I had no appetite. A small shop directly behind us was selling water and iced drinks. Water would do me good.

The shop was cool and seemed completely oblivious to the war. Immediately I thought of the little shop in the village where we would holiday every year. The smell of sweets. The massive variety of goods, cards, stickers and funny plugs that might be useful for recharging multiple phones. The lady behind the counter was just made to run a village shop, all mental arithmetic and kindliness. The person in front of me was chatting in that local-with-all-the-time-in-the-world manner that ignores other customers without actually meaning too. The effect was calming, an oasis. I felt at home and could have stood there all day in the cool, smelling the sweets and remembering one penny chews and liquorice Flyers. Yes, I thought, it was in a shop like this that I first purchased those precious liquorice Flyers.

The kind lady's eyes flashed with horror as I presented my two chilled bottles of water and a Ukrainian bank note that I thought should cover it. Turns out the note was about a day's wages! She carefully prised the wallet from my hands and removed two grubby little notes that she had seen me hide away. Just a few pence in value. A very kind and honest lady. I later discovered that her daughter had been raped by Russian soldiers when the village was occupied.

Back outside, I re-joined the rest of the team. The morning had been a jolt. 24 hours had seen us move from a five-star hotel to the furnace of the Donbas. Igor ran through where we were headed next. The name of the place sent an instant wash of adrenaline through me. It was on the front line. Not just in the Donbas or the red zone. The front line. We had a great deal to unload. Time to refocus.

Another hour on the road. We pulled into a garage so bombed out and wrecked that the sight of two functioning pumps on the forecourt seemed impossible. Yet there they stood - two miracle-white monoliths pumping fuel against all odds. Stepping out of our vehicle the shade of what was left of the roof gave way to burning sun with every other step. The shrapnel shredded covering hovered like an evil doily above us. Weird shafts of sunlight powered to the ground making visibility strangely difficult.

I almost bumped into a monster of a man with his pit bull rhinoceros hybrid of a dog. He just gave me a massive smile and wanted to high five. The dog was also far too friendly for its appearance. In a place where real aggression is in abundance, it always amazes me how calm and tolerant people are. We had a lovely conversation in English, and he thanked me for coming to help Ukraine. At that moment I was joined by Yaro and Mania who started interviewing the man. I think he was a senior local commander!

The coffee in the petrol station was another surprise. Workmen had already fixed the bathrooms and back-office area. The latest installation was a rather grand machine which was dutifully producing lattes, cappuccinos and a veritable

juke box of coffee-based drinks. Only months before the area
had been occupied by Russia. Already the reconstruction was
starting. What could be salvaged was being salvaged. What
needed replacing was being replaced as best it could. The look
on the garage owner's face said it all. She was going to trade
her way back to normality. Looking at the queue for coffee she
might just achieve that on latte sales alone!

Our military escort arrived. More coffees! I was happy
because that meant – for once – I would get to finish mine.
Their interpreter began explaining what would happen over
the next few hours. He then turned to me and repeated
the instruction in perfect English. Previously he had been
working as an interpreter for the New York Times. Under
escort we moved onto a tree-lined road that stretched into the
distance. After a few minutes we reached a check point. Once
through we would effectively be at the front line. The military
controlled area.

We drove on for another few kilometres and then stopped
on a patch of shaded concrete that had once been a bus station.
It was time to put on the body armour and helmets. And so
began the quiet ritual of checking ballistic plates, field dressing
bandages and tourniquets. All carried out with varying
degrees of OCD-level anxiety. I noticed that amongst our
group particular attention was paid to the positioning of lucky
mascots and badges that serve to personalise body armour
vests. For some, me included, these rituals serve to calm the
nerves and create an imaginary shield powered by those icons,
badges and beads. There is of course no logic to this but if it
serves a calming purpose, then that is all that matters. At the
time everything makes sense, including this stone age level of
superstition.

The weight of body armour is always a shock. You
suddenly gain ten kilos. Throw on some pouches and med kit

and you gain another four kilos. Put on the ballistic helmet that is another two kilos. You do feel safer. What you sacrifice is agility and in the high heat of summer a fair degree of ventilation too. Hydration becomes an important component in staying operationally effective. Looking around the group I noticed Anatoliy had declined to wear his armour. He gave me a look as if to say, "Meh! If your time is up, your time is up." I smiled in respect of his philosophy. He knew the risks. It is a free country. He also knew we had three tonnes of food to shift by hand in 40-degree heat.

The country lane beside us was a racetrack. Funkily camouflaged SUVs would flash past at crazy speeds. Armour would clatter through our position, engines straining with terrific gear shifts and smoke to achieve maximum velocity. It was time to move. We had been stopped (under tree cover, it must be said) for five minutes. Too long. There was a reason the trucks raced past us. Jumping in our vehicles we joined the survival drag race and headed for our next RV.

The previous destruction we witnessed on the road that morning was sadly only a primer for the twisted, Dadaist world we were now entering. Most infrastructure of note no longer existed. Concrete bridges of unimaginable mass lay dumped like dead dragons across entire roads. We were forced to detour onto tracks that, months before, had been no more than a bridle path. Factories sat crumpled in on themselves, deflated roofs rippled for hundreds of metres. The relentless and merciless nature of the pounding was humbling. The volume of rubble, cracked and busted into prehistoric lumps of rebar and cement manifested a dreamy sense of belittlement and weakness, fear and wonder in equal measure.

Entering the outskirts of our destination things became a little bit more cheerful. A few civilians were on the streets, people were shopping. One or two cafés were open. Some leafy lanes even looked quite cosy. Altogether the look and feel was more akin to a distressed town in Provence rather than a town on the front line of a massive war. Parking near a store area, we were greeted very warmly by the mayor and other local dignitaries. Across from the store council workers were strimming and cleaning the road and paths. The citizens of this place were clearly determined to keep their town in the best possible working order. After the last few hours, it was very moving and inspiring to see such civic pride. A lovely old boy came up and shook my hand, he wanted to help us shift the goods. My lip started wobbling for the first time that day.

Minutes later I discovered a very effective cure for wobbly lip syndrome: shifting tons of supplies, by hand, onto pallets, wearing body armour. Even if I had been crying no one would have noticed as I staggered, drenched in comedic levels of sweat. I was part of a human chain stacking slabs of tins onto a pallet. It was becoming hard to see through the salty fragrance of perspiration and melted sunblock washing down my face.

There was only one thing for it. Break out the "sweat rag." Believe it or not, the British Army issues a rather useful bit of clothing which is officially called "sweat rag." In Iraq I had come to love its comfort and utility. First in Basra, now in the Donbas - the military equivalent of a comfort blanket. Experience has taught me that the rag works best tied around my head, Rambo fashion. Once in place I could work safely again, sweat no longer blinding me.

What I was not fully aware of (at the time) was the unbridled mirth the act of wearing the rag would cause. The laughter attracted Yaro and Mania looking for an "angle." I presented the perfect "And finally" moment in the form of an eccentric Englishman, puffing and lobster red. Camera in my face I explained what we were doing in broken Polish. I hoped I had come across on film as the poet warrior of my delusions.

What was actually recorded for the Polish public was a sweaty, middle-aged man with something wrapped around his head. It was not a good look. The Poles and Ukrainians watching the piece must have thought is this the best that Great Britain can do? The overall impression was of a wheezing, stumbling eccentricity. They were some of the kinder remarks anyway.

Unloading completed, it was photo op time. I removed the headband and took my place with the rest of the team. Getting our breath back and surveying the hand-filled pallets, we felt justifiably proud. Knowing that supplies were now safely delivered was a wonderful feeling. The local people could now relax knowing that for the next week at least they would be more comfortable. A few less things to worry about can seem like a luxury in an uncertain world.

The mayor asked us if we wanted to look around the town. Despite the danger it seemed rude not too. We first followed him down to what was left of the hospital. Massive gaps in the building suggested the remains of waiting rooms and operating theatres. Multiple floors were exposed like a hideous doll's house. I stood next to a man who had been there at the time of the attack. He looked at me and I really did not know what to say. He then looked away nodding, reliving a private memory, wrapped in a past that will never leave him. The summer wind filtered through the trees. Birds sang and fought over insects. The strange peace of the immediate moment was of little solace to that man or the many others gathered with us.

From the hospital we walked in smaller groups to more open ground. Old buildings, new buildings, houses, schools all bore the scars and damage inflicted by tanks and artillery. The battle to liberate this place had been intense. One beautiful structure caught my attention. Almost Victorian in architecture, the building stood half destroyed with an exposed first floor. Christmas decorations still clung to what was left of a ceiling that appeared to float in mid-air. They were the sort of decorations children make together in school, all glue and paper stuck on the wrong way round. A fun project in the build-up to Christmas. The last Christmas that many of those children would ever see.

We moved on to a once beautiful park. Despite the devastation, somehow there was still a tattered dignity to the place. The trees had taken a hammering but were doing their best to provide shade. Benches still offered comfort despite high velocity holes in the metal work. The damage was considerable and expensive. Yet it was very clear that the park had been cleaned up with great care and love. This was a special place for the people of this town, a library of memories. You had the strong sense that over the years people had fallen in love here, bought balloons and ice cream, walked with grandparents and worried about exams. A future past. The park felt completely haunted by these happy times, which despite the damage, gave you the feeling that this is where you would instinctively come on a Sunday afternoon. But not now. The interpreter's arm pointed through the park and into the middle distance. There before us lay Mordor.

A seething horizon of smoke. A view which had to be metabolised first. The scene beyond comprehension in its panoramic shock. The intimidating scale tricked the eye into focusing on everything and nothing and back to everything again. It was as though we were standing on the rim of a great volcano, peering across a living, hissing expanse of destruction.

The interpreter pointed out spectacular splashes of fire, explaining the meanings and ranges of the different smoke columns. He spoke calmly and authoritatively as though we were on an artillery safari.

"Look, look over there, those are 155s working. Hey, hey, you see the black smoke billowing up over there?

That's a vehicle being hit." There, before us, a living diorama shifted and moved in a demonstration of massive kinetic exchange. It was both fascinating and horrifying. I remember thinking there was something rather 19th century about the experience. In 1815 many of the great and good observed Waterloo from a safe distance. Gettysburg and many other battles had their spectators too. The subsequent industrialisation of war had made battle watching a rather dangerous activity. Looking around the park I wondered if we were not being a little too cavalier. The scene, though, was mesmerising.

All my life I have been fascinated by military history. Never in my wildest dreams did I think I would ever see such a vista. From left to right as far as the eye could see, the future of Europe was being decided. Colossal explosions would appear drawing your eyes to another group of trees or factory buildings. Acrid smoke drifted towards us rotten with oil, chemicals and goodness knows what else. This is what total war looks like. A boiling, menacing confusion of noise, concussion waves and smoke.

It was odd, later on, to discover that the photographs we took looked misty and captured nothing of the supernatural atmosphere of what we witnessed. They could be foggy pictures of a landscape taken anywhere, devoid of our feelings or the real drama. The main problem is that real fire and explosions are not as spectacular as in the movies. Not as well choreographed. A real shell landing looks like a big puff of dirt. What films cannot convey is the powerful compression of the air, the shock waves that kill without leaving a scratch. Or the fact that from within that big puff of dirt, fly invisible one and two kilo chunks of steel that unravel from the shell casing at thousands of km and hour, scything through anything and everything until its kinetic energy is spent.

Anatoliy handed me a lump of jagged steel, the weight of a small dumbbell and with edges like knapped flint. I imagined it hitting a human body. The best you could hope for was a severed leg or arm. Pressing the shrapnel against my leg (in a vague attempt to understand its power) I realised that even buildings and bunkers would struggle to offer protection against such a razor-sharp mass flying at incredible velocity. As for the human body? Chance was your best defence.

Yet it was also a strange moment of cognitive dissonance. Anatoliy had found the shrapnel metres from where we were standing. Granted it was rusty and not red hot, meaning it was not fresh. Granted our military minders were very careful, managing just how close their charges were allowed to be in relation to this, the most horrific show on earth. However, it was now time to step back a little from the abyss. If nothing else to ensure we remained witnesses rather than become voyeurs, or more importantly casualties ourselves.

Krystian and I walked back through the park together with a Ukrainian soldier. Almost immediately it felt as though the volume of danger was being turned down. It was then we noticed what we both thought was a scaffolding pole sticking out of the ground at a jaunty angle. Before we could even investigate the soldier was grabbing us like two toddlers by a pond.

"Rocket, mate, unexploded."

It was not a very spectacular rocket, we were assured, but it was certainly still capable of spoiling our day. The soldier pointed to the extraordinary remains of a nearby metal bin. A similar rocket had turned said bin into what looked like a bad statue of a large bird spreading its wings.

"Don't touch things, please," said the soldier firmly and politely.

He gently herded us back through the park and towards the rest of the group who were some way ahead of us. The hypnotic spell of staring into the maelstrom broken, I realised Krystian and I may have spent slightly longer than intended at the observation point. The soldier seemed relieved by our compliance and haste when it came to catching up with the others. We were now only too happy to move further away from the edge and into the perceived safety of the town. Yaro and Mania were filming about ten metres away.

I noticed a slender object with a metallic tip right by my foot. I froze. My brain flashed through all the nightmarish possibilities of what the thing could be, none of them good. Half remembered aide memoires concerning unexploded ordnance gave way to memories of Sir John Mills in "Ryan's Daughter" holding a sand covered box of detonators. Yes!! That's what this was, a detonator!

"Detonator! I think there's a detonator by my foot," I said with unwarranted assurance. Thanks to Sir David Lean I was now apparently an expert on explosives.

Yaro and Krystian gingerly moved towards me. Yaro looked at the detonator, then looked back at me, stamping on the object with his great hoof. Before I had time to say, "What the hell are you doing?" he said, "Cigarette."

Examining the remains in the dirt it was indeed one of those cocktail cigarettes of a type that were considered very sophisticated in the 1980s. The filter was covered in metallic gold paper which to the ill-informed person might just look like one of the detonators in "Ryan's Daughter." A little bit.

So, the mystery of the "detonator" was resolved. My credibility as an identifier of explosive hazards was in the toilet. The bigger mystery was, who on earth was smoking cocktail cigarettes in 21st century war- torn Donbas? The soldier came over to ascertain what fuss was all about. The cocktail cigarette incident clearly proved that I had renewed my vows as the class clown.

Our soldier was a very cheerful chap. He reminded me of that one person you find in every IT department who just helps you without the sighing sarcasm. Confident and slightly shy at the same time, he talked of army life in the gauche, deflective way men describe a hobby they love but do not really want to talk about. He was much more interested in chatting about sport, food and family. We also talked about the future. I sometimes wonder if talking about the future in Ukraine is taboo. Are we tempting fate by talking about peace? Normal jobs? Or a Sunday sitting in that park without worrying about a random five kilos of heavy metal sparking across the flagstones and ripping someone to pieces?

We were led into a cellar which became a bunker that opened out into a series of meeting rooms. Each room contained people seated at desks or on phones. A busy, strangely normal subterranean scene. Igor and the gang were already in one meeting room alongside the mayor. Krystian and I were hastily ushered in and immediately a presentation ceremony began which Yaro and Mania filmed. It was one of those moments where you suddenly must be on your best behaviour. There was much hand-shaking and we were each presented with a beautiful book detailing the campaign and subsequent liberation of the region. We were being honoured by the leaders of that liberation and by those who stood up to Russia against incredible odds. The wobbly lip arrived right on cue as the mayor thanked the UK for all they were doing for Ukraine.

The underground infrastructure was formidable but also welcoming. From this location the seat of local government was being maintained. The bureaucracy was hugely impressive and very well organised. Members of the public were being handled in a calm professional way, waiting in the dim light, leaning on sandbagged entrances. The locals themselves were cheerful, polite and happy to see us. There was a very strong sense of community and purpose. Together the people and the authorities were going to re-build their town. What I saw was direct democracy in action.

The town must function as normally as possible (subject to unexploded ordnance being cleared). Flower beds were being tended, lawns mown, verges strimmed. At no point did one get the impression that standards were being allowed to slip because there was a war on. I never thought that a well-weeded flowerbed could be such an act of defiance but that is exactly what it was. Ukraine was showing the world a model functioning civic society – and only a few kilometres from the frontline.

Following the ceremony, we were driven to a restaurant, the sort of family run café you expect to find on a Mediterranean road trip rather than in a war zone. An oasis of happy diners and smiles. In true Ukrainian style there were delicious, seasoned meats, soups, bread, salads, kompot, fresh yoghurt, enough food for double the number of people at the table. The venue felt very cool, relaxing and safe. Quite an achievement in forty-degree heat with military vehicles racing past and crumps in the distance.

It was time to get back on the road. We had to go down to the very south of Ukraine that night. The mayor seemed shocked at the distances we were planning to cover. Alternative routes were discussed. Electronic maps switched on. I left the route map debate and thought this the perfect opportunity to fly the flag for the UK confectionary industry. Producing the liquorice Flyers I handed them out to our bewildered hosts. They liked them!! The only people in Ukraine to genuinely appreciate these quintessentially British sweets!!

Our new route took us down some very dark lanes and tracks. Maps near the front line worry me, mainly because they shift. Also because you do not have to drive very far the wrong way to be targeted by a drone or artillery. At one point we found ourselves rolling down a dusty lane, overgrown with trees that formed a tunnel of green. Direct sunlight converted the dry dust into an earthy fog of vehicles and soldiers. The ultra focused industry of the troops around us suggested we were very close to the front line. At one point I saw a self-propelled artillery position within metres of the track.

Silence reigned in our vehicles as we dutifully followed our escorts and bumped along a woodland track. In times of peace this shaded dell would have seemed enchanting. In that moment, the pure danger of where we were felt almost tangible. I felt closer to the edge than in the park. From this point the Russians were as close as they had ever been to our convoy. As that track meandered back onto a better road, I felt nothing but the most profound respect for those tough, dirt-coated men who were working all hours to keep the Russians at bay. Glancing into one of the side mirrors I saw their position rapidly swallowed up by the shade and green cover. No longer visible, I prayed that nature's camouflage would keep them safe.

Back on the open road we left the military zone and motored onto a main route south. The immense fields were being harvested by great parades of combine harvesters. I thought of my Grandpa's farm, and how the funny little harvester that came to buzz around our few acres compared to this endless hoovering of the land. One of those Ukrainian machines could have harvested everything on our farm in about an hour, including the buildings!

The sky and light are different in Ukraine too. The big sky of the steppe exposes everything. There is a feeling of nowhere to hide. For hours you can drive and see nothing but sky and golden corn, like the flag of Ukraine itself. Then suddenly you see an immense field with nothing but the flags of Ukraine. The fluttering markers of sacrifice and bravery.

One such field of flags was so vast that the convoy involuntarily slowed down. Igor's vehicle came to a halt. We all followed suit. I remember Krystian clambering onto the roof of the truck and just staring in disbelief. It was a reflex action induced by incomprehension. I am sure that no one reading this will have ever seen anything quite like this field. A sight that compelled me to say a quiet prayer. A sight that we thought Europe had promised never to permit again.

I have no idea how long we stopped by that terrible field. I just remember the flame-like roaring sound of the flags in the wind. What I can say is that other than the order to move no one spoke for at least half an hour once we were back on the road. Words failed all of us at that field. I can describe that bombed-out cafe, I can describe the little towns, the miles of smashed infrastructure and everything else from that day. I will never be able to describe the mortal tragedy, scale and emotion of that field. Each flag represented the private and collective suffering of Ukraine.

Heading into the late afternoon sun, I began to compensate for what we had seen by imagining what we could do to Russia and Russians. I thought about everything evil that Russia had done. From my own dear Babcia's experiences right through to the millennium of suffering Moscow had inflicted on all its neighbours. It does not take very long to start considering all sorts of interesting options for a future Russia. Or rather a Russia without a future at all.

The remains of the afternoon passed into the warm light of a balmy evening. We stopped for a snack at a lovely little garage in the middle of nowhere. A nut-brown craggy-faced old man approached our vehicle and began unhooking the diesel pump. When he saw the rest of the convoy pulling up he smiled the smile all small business owners must make when a windfall closes the day. We chatted in a mixture of Polish and general Slavic words. I may well be at the forefront of developing a new Slavic Esperanto. I am quite convinced he understood everything I said and that I understood everything he said. Or maybe the rather large fuel bill persuaded him that it may be better to humour the foreign bloke with nods and smiles.

Sitting by the little café area we enjoyed our fresh coffee. My goodness, the Ukrainians do the very best garage coffee. The quiet of the evening allowed for the hum of distant farm machinery to be heard or the shouts as one grain truck was overfilled, the driver waving in irritation as he found himself with a unwanted creaking chassis. Alongside us, a Ukrainian soldier was meeting his kids. I got the impression they had not seen each other for quite some time. We respectfully cut the banter down to quiet conversation. Our noisy silliness could wait when compared to the precious moments a brave man was spending with his family. It was hard to ignore the raw emotion of the situation. He gave us a thankful smile as if to say, "Thank you for understanding what this moment means to me." We all smiled back and nodded in solidarity. Gathering our things, we quietly headed back to the trucks. Much rubbing of eyes and wobbly lips.

We arrived at our destination late at night. The streets were very quiet save for the odd trotting dog and rather strangely a very athletic man doing pull ups. He dropped down to wave at us and show his support. Our accommodation was a rather pleasant hostel and after a very long day it may be of no surprise to the reader that we were all asleep within minutes of checking in.

THE WAR NEXT DOOR

DAY 5

MY ROOMMATE, ANATOLIY, was already up, half
dressed and pointing at me and the shower, smiling. Minutes
later we were heading down to breakfast. Anatoliy leaned
over the balcony almost right outside our door and motioned
what a long way down it was. I edged past. We giggled as
I explained that heights are just about my number one fear
that has got worse with age. I always had slight vertigo which
turned into a fully fledged issue, thanks to a glass elevator in
Singapore about ten years ago.

Breakfast was a spicy, colourful, cheesy scrambled egg
combination which Anatoliy ordered under his breath as
though it were the greatest secret in all of Ukraine. The waiter
nodded in a similar conspiratorial fashion. The rest of the
team joined us in time to be presented with plates of the super
calorific omelette. Everyone agreed it was a good idea. Igor
compounded this by saying that we would have our toughest
day today and would need the energy. He said it very calmly, in
the manner of a time-served farmer who reads the weather by
feel and gets it right every time.

The journey to the coast took all morning. A cheerful start
was eradicated in an instant as we suddenly found ourselves
passing a roadside horror being cleaned up by the authorities.
The scene was grim. The vehicles slowed to a crawling speed,
adrenaline washing through all of us with a cliff-dive intensity.
One moment you are all jokes, the next confronting a butcher's
yard of death and bewilderment.

A powerful memory came back to me. A roadside
moment from so very long ago. Embedded in the soundtrack
of that memory I could hear my section commander Billy's
Glaswegian voice: "No rubbernecking now!"

It came as an order, one morning in Basra. We had found

ourselves passing the semi-decapitated remains of an executed
Ba'ath Party grandee. Whether I want to or not, I can still see
what was left of the man's head, a memory photo that cannot
be deleted. All these years later, I would like to think that I
had learned my lesson and heeded old Billy's advice: "If you do
not need to see, then do not look."

I fought it, yet from the corner of my eye, on that
Ukrainian road, I half saw lumps and gore being moved.
Enough to make me nauseous but not enough to create an
indelible image. At least I hope not. I cannot be sure of what I
saw.

We drove on. I popped a comforting liquorice Flyer into
my mouth and allowed myself a moment to let the sugar deal
with the nausea. I find a sugary piece of something after a
shock very calming. Maybe there is a clinical reason for this,
or it could just be psychosomatic? Relatively harmless self-
medication works for me.

We all registered the quiet tragedy in our own way.
Nothing needed to be said. Stating the obvious did not
seem appropriate. You do not knowingly attend a football
match and then act surprised if people start kicking a ball.
A respectful shock gradually gave way to focusing on our
mission. We had a long day ahead of us.

We were approaching the outskirts of a battered city we
visited last year. In the previous December the dreary winter
light had somehow hidden much of the destruction. The harsh
sun now cast strange, irregular shadows that served to expose
any damage and shed light where architecturally there should
be none. Yet as with everywhere in Ukraine, people were out
and about, having a coffee, chatting by the bomb shelters,
delivering parcels and just generally getting on with their day.

Once we had passed through the city we headed deeper
into the recaptured coastal region. Only then did you feel the

weight of the military and the danger. The countryside was different too. If the Donbas approximates to a rolling southern French landscape, this area had a flatter almost desert-like feel. The light was different too, so powerful that it seemingly bounced back up at you, reflected by the bleached ground, married with an unforgiving heat. Sunglasses were a necessity.

There was a feeling of exposure too. Our chosen route passed through open marsh grasses as far as the eye could see. Storks and herons sat waiting, oblivious in a golden sea. A bird watcher's paradise in happier times. Anatoliy pointed to the land on the other side of the gulf and just said, "Bad guys."

The far shore instantly became more menacing, now a foreboding khaki sliver shimmering in the heat. It was hard to gauge the distance. I hoped the Russians were finding it equally hard to gauge the range and that the flooding and chaos of recent weeks had disrupted them, pushing them back further from that water's edge.

Igor was already scanning the horizon with binoculars. No movement could be seen. That was not necessarily encouraging as things are often only seen because they move. Battle hardened soldiers will only move in daylight when they have to, or when a target of opportunity appears. It was time to shift before we became that target. If you move you are easier to see, if you are stationary, you are easier to hit. Tough choices.

We emerged from the reed grass into an open area. Before us lay a smashed cove of destroyed Russian armour that cuddled the natural bay. Vehicles and tanks heaped together in semi-cover, seeking shelter from oblivion. It had been a turkey shoot. The last, desperate moments of tanks and armoured personnel carriers were evidenced by the jaunty angles and the self-preserving, clambering nature of where they lay. The ground was burnt into a crunchy black halo around them. No escape for the occupants. A mechanical Pompeii.

JULY CONVOY

The scorching summer wind caused the flimsier metal debris to plink and rattle in lifeless gusts, the strange rhythms of a knocking, pendulous destruction. Rusty wire and battered ammunition boxes drumming against lumps of blistered rusting steel made for ghostly atonal music. The faint aroma of oil-burnt earth and human decay would push past us with each hairdryer rush of wind.

As we moved closer to our destination I noticed how the soldiers were increasingly worn and salty, hard-earned efficiency and utility married with that lean look of men and women living in the field. Their equipment personalised and stripped down to the bare essentials. We must have looked eccentric at best as they waved us down to check who we were and where we were going.

Partly out of curiosity and partly out of concern. I suddenly got the feeling we were now as close to a front line as we had ever been on any of these convoys. One could sense the "Well, if you are mad enough to be here, then you must be one of us," instant camaraderie radiating from the soldiers. We discovered one had worked for years in Poland, his eyes gleaming with fond memories of peaceful times and sending money home. He shook his head with a never-thought-it would-come- to-this abandon and for some reason it made a shiver go down my spine. Poland suddenly felt a very long way away.

Igor then mentioned who we were meeting and instantly a wave of mythical respect bristled through the troops. The mere mention of the man's name was like a magic word elevating them to a new level of understanding of who we were. It served to make me more nervous. Who on earth was this man? The mere mention of his name made him seem like a Colonel Kurtz, war-prophet figure. I drew comfort from the fact that he appeared to be loved rather than feared but that is all relative in the vortex of war.

Secretive directions lead us down streets that had all but ceased to exist. Landmarks and instructions became as basic as turn left at the oil drum with three holes and then drive about a hundred metres till you find a pile of melted bicycles. House after house lay swept into the road by endless barrages, creating claustrophobic tributaries where there had once been an avenue. Nothing could have survived. Then a miracle house would emerge, almost untouched by the lottery of total war. We turned left. We turned right. We brushed under half-fallen trees and carefully drove over massive cables. The apocalyptic maze overwhelmed my sense of direction.

Finally, we came to a halt. In the silent road I was aware of a gate opening painfully slowly on bomb-warped hinges. Before we had time to help, an elderly lady emerged, all dignified smiles and kindness. Tania was the archetypical granny, babushka and Babcia all rolled into one. She just stood with love and defiance in what was left of her street. I really wanted to cry. No bog standard wobbly bottom lip this time, proper funereal crying.

I thought of my Babcia stuck in this place, fighting to survive, fighting to feed herself. Thankfully, Igor and Krystian greeted her, allowing me to snivel and hide around the back of one of the trucks, pretending to check fastenings and look for any damage. I managed to control my breathing enough to stop crying. It was like an emotional emergency stop, my sobbing skidded to a halt whilst the trusty sweat rag became my trusty tear rag. I composed myself enough to follow the group into what was left of her compound.

Then Tania surprised us by asking us to wash our hands before lunch!

This town had had no running water for over a year yet somehow Tania had rigged up the most wonderful Heath Robinson plumbing system of twisting pipes and tape and then more twisting pipes. It was ingenious, so much so that it stopped me blubbing. Tania demonstrated that her water system began with an old toilet cistern. The cistern would be filled by hand and then flushed. Gravity would then push the water around the old existing plumbing. A turn of a tap revealed a respectable trickle and delighted everyone.

Whilst we washed our hands, Tania explained that both houses on either side of her home had been destroyed. Only one other family now lived in her street. They waved at us through grape vines and fruit trees across the way. Much of her garden had yet to be cleared by EOD (mine clearance specialists) She pointed at some apple trees that were out of bounds. Their forbidden fruit tempting and juicy in the sunlight.

Heading into her home, a loud CRUMP erupted in a distant field close enough to make us all flinch.

"Meh," said Tania almost appalled at the shell's pathetic lack of conviction. "I bet it's that's that gun over there." She waved vaguely in the direction of the gulf and looked at our minder. "I wish they would do something about it," she added, in the casually irritated manner of someone complaining about pot holes to a neighbour. Tania's neighbours were dead though.

Walking across her small yard, she pointed out a narrow set of stairs that led to a shelter room deep underground and just big enough to sleep in. In the past its purpose was a natural cold store for preserved fruits. Never did she think it would preserve her life. She spun around daintily and pointed to the smashed remains of her neighbours' house on the other side of her property. All this destruction happened as she shivered on the earthen floor of her cold store. Tania then pointed out the path of a shell that had passed right through her property, gouging out a cauterised rift right across her ceiling.

I peered into the cold store. It was a grave of a hole, the walls so close that your voice was instantly absorbed by the black earth. No one would hear you scream. A frightening, dark, claustrophobic place. On a bright sunny day tolerable for a few minutes. For a little, lonely old lady under the Somme-like barrage of the previous year, it must have seemed like the end of days. I motioned my sympathy by clasping my hands to my heart and Tania just grinned and said, "Meh! Come and have some lunch."

She had prepared a great feast for us. The town had no electricity and no running water, yet Tania produced beautifully baked fresh bread and fresh cakes. A plate of homemade butter and a lovely soup was placed in front of us, all made on ancient stoves, using techniques that she remembered as a little girl.

The mod cons of the modern kitchen were useless in this shattered town. There were no shops. Food now had to be sourced and prepared from scratch. Women like Tania grew up in the shadow of the Holodomor (the Stalin-induced famine that killed millions of Ukrainians in the Thirties) and had their childhood disrupted by the Second World War. In a weird way, despite her frailty, maybe she was better placed to metabolise the nightmare world around her. She had begun her life in total war. Now in the winter of her days total war had returned. The muscle memory of survival kicked in to meet the current hardships, with a hard-earned stoicism.

I stared out of the ancient window frame, all reinforced with layers of paint and DIY innovation. Tania had begun fixing up her property the moment the fighting had finished. My eyes welled up as I thought of my Babcia and how similar Tania and old Babcia were. The same drive and unconscious thrift, the same love too. Tania was in my face with a big smile, offering more of the heavenly bread and butter. She had that motherly look of, " You are not crying are you?"

I asked her how close Polish was to her language.

"Oh, I understand most Polish, it's so similar to Ukrainian, we can understand each other. I even understand you speaking Polish too."

At that point Krystian chipped in and they were off to the races about life, what Tania needed and how we could help. Thank you, Krystian, for giving me the space to compose myself!!

After lunch, we unloaded the food and implements that Tania had requested from a previous convoy. The surviving neighbours came over from across the street and the sharing began. It was a humbling scene. The level of interaction went beyond community – it was tribal survival. The Russians had reduced these people to living in a post-apocalyptic world. On the one hand there was a terrible beauty in the way these neighbours had come together, determined to live and support each other. On the other hand, I could not help feeling an extraordinary anger. Decent, ordinary, loving people had been reduced to living a stone age existence. If only the over-indulged and arrogant Russians of St Petersburg and Moscow could see what they had done to people who did not have very much in the first place. Would they care?

A man emerged from nowhere. From the body language of the locals, it was clear he was loved and respected in equal measure. He had that look of instant competence, of making things happen. Igor hugged him. They exchanged whispered messages in the time it took to embrace. All done in the manner of a football captain secretly counselling a player before the referee does. The man came and shook my hand and instantly made me feel better. Dimitri was one of the leaders of the local resistance. He had quite a story to tell.

First, we had more kit to unload, all manner of tools,

machines and generators. If the town was to survive, then little by little it would have to be built back or at best maintained. Once we had finished, Dimitri asked if we wanted to have a look around the town. With his guidance, we could follow the path of the battle that had seen the Russians defeated and pushed a few kilometres away.

I have written before that military tourism can be a ghoulish pastime, often frowned upon by soldiers who end up having to rescue idiots posing with a burned-out tank. However, the opportunity to be walked through a barely cold battlefield, by one of the partisans who prosecuted the battle, was an opportunity that we had to take. We drove to another part of town to hide our vehicles and set out on foot. Dimitri paused and briefed us about safety, only tread where I tread, do not pick anything up and be situationally aware. The Russians were still only a few kilometres away.

We began in the back yard of a ruined house. I vividly remember a set of children's bicycles, ranging from toddler to teenager, burned yet neatly stacked against a wall, the exposed springs of the seats and melted stabilisers, ready for a skeletal bike ride. We pushed past the remains of a kitchen, dry pasta spilling out from a cupboard, plates still on the draining board. The front garden path led onto a road. A main gate lay blasted by incredible force, sheet steel crushed like tin foil wrapped around a pebble. The front of the house had taken the rest of the explosion, shrapnel digging deep flowery strike marks, starting at the front door and ending through the splintered eaves of the roof. Once on the main road it was clear that every house the length of the street had been smashed, blown up or fought over with equal ferocity. This was just one street.

The heat of the afternoon was stifling. The wind breathed up and down the road almost as though giant bellows were pushing against us, moaning through the gaps in buildings. Sudden squalls wafting dust into our eyes.

Occasionally Dimitri would take a knee or drop behind a wall. He spoke with a bewildered, almost disbelieving, sincerity. How could this have happened? Weeks before he had been the head of PE at the local secondary school. Now he found himself aiming £250,000 Javelins at Russian tanks. A push of a button and the vehicle would "lollypop," throwing its turret and gun in a torrent of white heat and shredded flesh. He turned to me, marvelling at the physics.

"Ten tonne lollypop!" he said in English. I suspect the fitness and command that comes with teaching PE made him a natural choice in terms of leadership.

We continued down the street and the devastation became worse. The mountainous rubble told a story of a battle gathering in intensity about every twenty metres. It was hard to see how anything, or anyone could survive. The digger-deep blasts and scooping shards of shrapnel left no space for survival, as far as I could see. Much of the ground was also burnt, fired like clay in a kiln and glazed with oil and grease.

At the end of the road Dimitri gathered us together as though we were on the most normal guided tour in the world. On the opposite side of the junction sat a large building. It looked like it had been dropped from a great height, all buckled foundations and twisted lintels.

"This is my school," Dimitri stated with great pride. His use of the present tense very moving.

We now had to be very careful. The school had been the epicentre of the recent fighting. The relative ease of walking down the road gave way to a single file trek along a cleared path to the school.

To the left of the path sat half the chassis of a BMP 2 troop carrier. Ten metres further on lay a coiled lump of track, resembling a giant, badly wrapped tape measure. A massive, jagged piece of aluminium was wedged into the ground. The front of the BMP was now up standing in a precarious neolithic style. A metal menhir. Beyond that buzzed the remains of one of the occupants. The body lay lumped in the undergrowth. Tossed like a rag doll by the exploding BMP. Flies and filth collected at certain points on what was left of the dead Russian. Thanks to that strong wind the smell was bearable.

Our group moved on. I remember being more concerned about keeping up with the team than the sight of that soldier's body. We crossed a little homemade bridge that traversed a trench containing boots, and greasy war waste that I did not care to look at. We followed Dimitri past what looked like the delivery area of the school. A brand new, smashed courier van lay splayed like a half-opened flower in a bed of breeze blocks, decorated with shattered glass. In a window space directly above that van a dead barn owl hung in a lifeless stretch, caught up in camouflage netting, a mournful, painful look still embedded on its face. If anything summed up the horror of the school, it was this owl.

The building had become something of an Alamo. Over one thousand people had died fighting in and around the premises. The feeling of violence was still palpable, with this level of destruction the danger remains. It might be an unexploded mortar round buried up to its tail, or a grenade wedged between some stones as a crude booby trap. It could also be as simple as a two hundred kilo chunk of concrete dangling from rusty wire mesh biding its time in the knocking wind. A veritable sword of Damocles for the unsuspecting.

Thankfully our guide and protector Dimitri pointed out these hazards and pitfalls. He did it in the cheerful manner of someone who has just inherited an unruly garden, pointing to a lump of metal and saying with a grin, "Not sure what that is but let's give it a wide birth and move on."

The safe sheep path led us to another entrance that had been completely removed, including the stone steps. The doorway now hovered at a height that appeared ridiculous. Access was now via a pile of theatre chairs. They were of a similar model to the ones used by that unit in the Donbas. Gingerly, we began climbing the pile. The sensation was like participating in a giant game of chair Jenga. The creaking and flipping of seats created an unnerving soundtrack, accompanied by multilingual swearing and nervous laughter. As the doorway came within reach Dimitri and Krystian grabbed me and pulled me through the breach. Looking back down the pile it was clear that the return journey was going to be a bigger challenge.

Pigeons flew in all directions as we scrambled into what had been the school gym.

"The floor is very solid in this part," stated Dimitri.

From a health and safety perspective this did not fill me with confidence. Having said that any thoughts of health and safety should have been packed away about four days previously. The floor was indeed solid but rendered hazardous by the thousands of spent AK 47 casings. Trapped under your boots, these rounds acted like mini-roller skates. It was easier to walk without picking your feet up, wading through a shallow sea of brass. A solitary pink child-size trainer sat on the floor. The wall bars of the gym were strangely intact, as was a basketball hoop that hung forlorn on the wall.

Dimitri peered around a corner and beckoned us to follow him. A strange and surprising rush of air greeted us. A gaping hole on the other side of the building channelled a breeze through a reception area, the condensing effect of an enclosed space accelerating the velocity of the hot air. For a moment we were stuck in a dust-driven wind tunnel, shielding eyes and mouths from the choking gale. A quick sidestep onto a staircase provided instant respite, save for the spooky moaning of the wind through endless bomb-created apertures.

We followed Dimitri up those stairs. The debris was so thick that often three or four steps at a time were buried to the point of being unusable. Faith had to be placed in rocking banisters and leaps forward in order to bypass the obstacle.

On the landing of what I believe was the second floor, Dimitri paused and allowed us to scan the horizon. Through the shimmering heat we could observe what remained of the town. It was another shock. The terrible damage looked worse from an elevated position. Uninhabitable. Homes levelled, Hiroshima style, to basic foundations and footprints. Plots marked out only by remaining stones and surviving fireplaces. The occasional lucky home clung onto civilisation, hastily nailed tarpaulins providing temporary flapping roofs. We gathered as a speechless group, the silence somehow magnifying our inability to comprehend the rubble stretched before us. A perspective reaching into oblivion.

Breaking the spell, Dimitri dragged us into a room filled with blocks and obstacles. At one end sat a beautiful cabinet with an intact mirror, surreal in its survival. We stared at our reflections, surprised by dusty faces and clothes, and maybe more so by the stress on those faces. We were all just that little bit less recognisable than we had been over breakfast. Was it the dust, caked on our faces like bad school play make up? Or were we absorbing the grief that haunted this crumbling nightmare of a building? Our eyes did not lie as they stared back at us wondering how we would feel if our hometowns had been vaporised.

Dimitri wanted to show us what was left of the school library. We crashed our way over debris piled so high the remaining ceiling almost met our heads. Some bookshelves had survived. A shelf of relatively pristine set texts sat waiting for collection. Other books had been turned into dusty pulp, ripped by shrapnel and melted into nuggets of papier-mâché by the spring rains.

The fighting in this building had been metre by metre, Stalingrad-style. A merciless battle for a building the size of your average town hall. It seemed so strange that a library should become the focus of such violence. Yet whoever controlled the library controlled the building. If you controlled the building, you controlled the town. "Libraries gave us power," as someone once said. Dimitri estimated that at least forty bodies remained under our feet. The equipment needed to recover them was not available. You clear and bury what you can with the resources you have.

The rest of the group were very keen to continue climbing and reach the top floor. This required leaping over a three-storey drop and grabbing onto a concrete door frame of dubious integrity. Before I could say, "This is not a good idea," Igor and others were jumping, grabbing and moving on with simian abandon.

I peered over the edge. The drop was almost identical in depth to the nausea-inducing balcony back at the hostel. I stepped back from the precipice. Daring myself to peep again, the twisted rebar and concrete below convinced me that the risk was just not worth the reward. Problem – to go back down through the building without Dimitri's guidance was probably as dangerous as the leap. I fretted like a toddler and was about to call out when Dimitri's face appeared round the corner.

"Come," he said, "jump, trust me." His demeanour was very calm and reassuring. He was every inch that confidence-building PE teacher, helping the weakest pupil achieve their physical best. "You can do this, I know you can."

The wind lifted his flowing locks and in that cinematic

moment he almost became my guardian angel. I felt absolved
of responsibility. Putting my complete trust in St Dimitri, I
crouched and jumped. St Dimitri reached for me, using the
energy of my clumsiness to throw me onto the concrete floor
on the other side. It was not a graceful move. We laughed in a
"bet you didn't think you would be doing that today" fashion
and caught up with the others.

Igor and the gang were already on the top floor, so badly
damaged that it gave one the impression of being on a flat
roof. Fully exposed to the warm winds, there was something
otherworldly about this classroom in the sky. The desks and
chairs still ordered against a bright blue afternoon, as though
part of a terrible dream. The view should have been beautiful.
I thought of the many kids who must have sat in this space,
staring out across the little town. They could probably see
their homes, their street, the neighbours, the road home. None
of that existed anymore. Only a desperate community of
survivors. A population of 2,500 reduced to a hundred people
clinging to life.

In the distance dark, sinister columns of black smoke
forced their way out of the ground. Dimitri announced he had
more to show us.

The route down through the building was the sort of speedy
slide and skid that is best attempted aged eleven. Thanks to
Dimitri's confidence-boosting instructions I was a little better at
keeping up with the gang. I even managed to leap back over the
chasm that had almost defeated me before. We seemed to be
back outside in no time and heading for our vehicles.

Bumping over uneven ground, we headed towards
the smoke that had seemed so distant from the top of the
school. Our route was a dirt track that ran alongside an
expansive wheat field. A combine harvester was consuming
the remaining crop. We all waved. The driver waved back.

The smell of corn dust transported me back forty years to my grandfather's farm. Harvest time. Even the lumpy track reminded me of the route to his great back field. It seemed like the biggest acreage in the world back then. Compared to the spaces of Ukraine, that old back field was a paddock.

Parking up under cover, Dimitri was already pacing towards a hedge row. We carefully followed the path he had taken and gathered around him. Under the cover of a strip of land that was part hedgerow, part linear copse, we moved forward. Dimitri pointed at a lop-sided tank and edged forward. The turret was completely blown off, landing badly onto one side of the tank.

"Javelin," said Dimitri.

I peeped into the main body of the vehicle. Nothing but burnt residue. The super heat of the Javelin round and subsequent explosion married crew with steel and the blistered interior. The odd shiny engine part gleamed, juxtaposed against the rust- and oil-bathed surrounding grass. Tweeting birds and the beautiful weather seemed completely oblivious to the recent violence. Swallows swooped and ducked under the tank's barrel, sling-shotting around its corroding mass, before disappearing into a cloud of insects.

Dmitri moved further along the copse row. Two Russian Tiger four-wheel drive trucks sat scorched, frozen in their last moments before the molten impact of a shell, the innards of the vehicles immolated beyond recognition. Body armour lay metres away, ripped to rags by the force of the blast. Melted boots and rifle magazines littered the area, the kit ever so slightly more robust than the biological owners.

The husk of a Russian APC (another BMP2) disintegrated nearby, had clearly carried on driving after being hit. Its erratic, driverless course, preserved in the dried mud, evidence of the dying moments before a secondary explosion ripped off the turret and brought the runaway vehicle to a halt. The turret lay over twenty metres away, buried in the ground as though fallen from a great height.

As we approached the APC, a startled barn owl spun from its perch in the blackened hull and took off in the direction of the enemy! Before leaving the owl gave us the angriest look I have ever seen from an animal. "Just **** off and leave me alone!," it would have said had the owl spoken English. I thought of its dead friend caught up in netting at the school. Even the poor owls could not escape the enveloping destruction of this war. He probably thought he was safe in that knocked out APC, lightening never striking twice. Then we came along.

Further along the tree line we found trenches and dug-outs. One had been blasted into an instant quarry by a well-placed 155 artillery shell. Others remained intact. Holes in the ground revealed half eaten meals and tin can detritus. There was an element of the Marie Celeste about the place. Fearing the worst and under poor leadership, I suspected these Russians had decided to jump into their vehicles and flee. It was the last thing that they would ever do. They would have been better off staying under cover.

The holes smelled of fear, urine and bonfires. Dimitri allowed us to peer in but go no further. Booby traps may still have been in place. Not so very long ago this had been the front line. The new front line was not so very far away either. That black smoke was much closer now. Igor even managed to film a ball of flame as something exploded about two km away. We all stood and stared, wearily disbelieving of the middle distance that boiled and erupted before us.

Dimitri let us look for a few seconds before leading us back along the carefully chosen trail. The ground was littered with live 12.7mm rounds, clumps of 7.62mm rounds, partially exposed like fossils in clods of earth. The ripped front part of a set of body armour sat just off the path, all shredded and burnt, the material micro frayed in the way that moths eat through an old suit. Moths tend not to have the same effect on the owner though.

Back with our vehicles, we waited under cover. The leafy canopy allowed Dimitri to assess the drone situation. Once clear, we moved back into the remains of the town. Dimitri was dropped off with a very quick goodbye, disappearing into the maze of rubble and cover.

Heading back the way we came we marvelled at the courage and tenacity of those that remained in that little town. They will never give up. Tania will continue to resist in her own way as Dimitri will in his.

Back on the road, our next stop was a medical facility. The busy highway a constant convoy of trucks and supplies. The Black Sea looked inviting in the evening sun, but we had more drops to make. Fatigue was kicking in too. Clambering over rubble, lifting boxes of supplies and the general stress of being in a war zone were cumulatively starting to affect morale. I think we all could have done without this final drop of the day - until we got to the location.

Exhausted medical staff just stared at us, too tired to smoke their cigarettes. Leaning on banisters and doorways, catching a momentary break of coffee, fresh air and nicotine whilst trying to fathom all they had seen. There was no conversation, no acknowledgement of us or even their own colleagues. This was a level of fatigue that bordered on a waking unconsciousness. The zombie spell was only broken when a senior surgeon called them back into theatre. In a flash of energy, the stasis instantly left them. Adrenalised and reanimated, they were resurrected in an instant. Once again, they became ultra-focussed medics, ready for yet another amputation or reassembly of damaged soldiers.

Shamed by witnessing their exhaustion, we soon had the trailers open. Forming a chain we shifted boxes of dressings, drips, needles and all manner of equipment into a storeroom. At one point, Krystian spoke to me in English. I remember a nurse staring at us, concentrating on our words, the half understanding in her eyes. I knew she wanted to say something in English. She also knew she could speak English but was just too tired to allocate her remaining energy into forming a sentence. A mad giggle and a wave of the hand was all she could muster. Nothing needed to be said anyway. Besides the wobbly bottom lip had returned and I knew that speaking for me meant blubbing.

Delivery complete, it was time to head north. The setting sun was now a beautiful red mass, bathing the west in a glow which seemed to be saying it was time to go home. In practical terms all equipment had been delivered. The convoy was complete.

I have a photo from that evening that evokes a powerful memory. The photo itself looks silly, innocuous even. It is an image of Anatoliy holding a latte in a brightly lit, Americana-themed café. Nothing apparently remarkable. Under normal circumstances such a picture would probably be deleted like millions of other meaningless digital snaps. And yet, this photo captures a moment of incredulity that briefly questioned our sanity. The gleaming roadside café, with its multiple choices of ice cream, coffee and cakes, the neon-lit cleanliness of the floors and marble tiles. We all thought it and vocalised it at the same time. "How can this be?"

In the space of one day, we had seen terrible destruction, death and the gruesome frontline of a horrible war. Those faces of traumatised hospital staff were as fresh in our minds as the pain au chocolate and skinny lattes in front of us. The smiling café staff were in cleaner uniforms than the medics we had seen hours before. I photographed Anatoliy in that moment. He is smiling, no, he is beaming. We were all beaming. Why? It was not just the relief of being away from the military zone. I have come to realise that in that moment the café represented hope, an achievable future that already existed in Ukraine. If a place like this could exist in the space that we were standing in, then it could exist in the space that Tania and Dimitri were standing in too.

That thought seemed very powerful and comforting at the time. Granted we were very tired, but I never imagined that a roadside café could initiate such powerful philosophising. The cosmetic presence of the café did more for our morale than just the coffee and cakes. Making full use of the gents, we washed the deep dirt from our faces and hands, fascinated by the varying colours and viscous lumps we dissolved from the film of grime that covered us. We silently watched the muck glug down those beautiful basins. Dark rivers of oil, grease and whatever else clung to our skin, the filth so powerful that it seemed to stain the glaze of the basins. We allowed the warm fresh water and liquid soap to run over our arms. A cleansing ritual, rubbing faces again and again until we became clean and recognisable. The filth on our clothes would have to wait. We tidied up the sinks as best we could, paper towels overwhelming the waste bin. A cleaning lady stood at the door, politely waiting for us to finish. She waved away our apologies.

"No worry, I make guess where you come from," she said in English with a warm smile of solidarity. I really needed that smile after the day we had had.

DAY 6

I AWOKE LATE. So late that something felt off. Voices from

the kitchen canteen sounded relaxed, lazy even. Someone else was singing in a bathroom. Laughter came from another room interrupting the unintelligible tones of an anecdote.

Were they waiting for me? I jumped out of my sleeping bag, pulled on a clean pair of trousers and dashed down the corridor. Fully expecting to be late for whatever we had planned for that day.

Krystian was sat at a table smiling. "You want omelette?"

"Will I have time to eat it?"

"Yes, we have day off," said Krystian.

A day off! Instead of the usual mad rush of drops and deliveries we were going to the local park and then on to Anatoliy's parents for a lovely meal.

The park was quite a surprise, beautifully landscaped and a luscious green. A total contrast from the golden perspective of the steppe that our eyes had grown used to over the last few days. It may as well have been another country. Developed in the 18th century, the parkland was reminiscent of a British stately home. The fountains and follies felt familiar, comforting even, their sculpted beauty wildly at odds with the jagged memories of the last few days. Calm and wonder settled over the group as we sat and observed the world going by. We had found a place where the war ceased to exist.

By the time we arrived at Anatoliy's house, his mother had filled a table full of food and was already cooking replacement dishes for the anticipated consumption. I offered to help but was ordered to sit at the rapidly filling table.

Then Anatoliy's cousin arrived. The room fell silent out of respect. A survivor of the Azov Steel plant, he had been captured and abused terribly by the Russians. Joining us at the table it was clear his injuries were still giving him tremendous pain as he navigated his way around the chairs. I found myself sitting next to him and carefully shook his hand. He asked me all sorts of questions about the UK and the process of gathering equipment for Ukraine. We discovered that we both spoke French and managed to silence the room as no one could work out what we were talking about. I later discovered that I was mixing Polish and French, so absolutely no-one understood what I was talking about!

The first of the toasts was called for. Following the Donbas moonshine experience of a few days previously I had rather hoped that there would be no more drinking.

Anatoliy glared at me. "Day off, day off," he chanted in mock disgust.

Before I had had a chance to comprehend the power of the vodka running down my throat, my glass was re-filled. Another toast. My fate was sealed.

My only advice to anyone caught in these pan-Slavic drinking situations (other than do not drink!) is that you must keep eating. Little and often. One shot must be countered with a piece of meat, bread or something that approximates the volume of the shot. The process will not stop you getting drunk, but it might just stop you from going to hospital.

By now the lunch had turned into a party. Anatoliy's brother arrived; others soon followed. The day was becoming a magical blur of laughter, stories and toasts. A momentum was building. By now I had lost count of the shots. We were into the realm of drinking where East most definitely does not meet West! I have tried over many years in Poland to gauge when to stop. I have come to realise it is not peer pressure that keeps you drinking, it is the fact that you are having too much fun.

Only Igor and Krystian refrained. Both are athletes and this level of drinking would probably knock them out of competition for weeks, all that hard-earned fitness gone in the misty vodka fog that enveloped the room.

"Come! We meet friends!" yelled Anatoliy.

Suddenly, we all seemed to be on our feet. Igor gave me a look as if to say, "Will, you are playing in the big league now, be careful".

We drove through the town, Igor and Krystian the obvious choices for designated drivers. Worryingly, there was a debate about this.

On route we discovered a terribly damaged tower block. A missile had struck weeks before killing many civilians. A makeshift monument, sat in front of the devastation. A collage of photos depicting the victims in happy moments. Granny on the beach, a little girl painting on a kitchen table, proud parents leaning into the photo.

Parking the vehicles, we approached the hideous void. The horror compounded by the intact, identical, apartment blocks surrounding the crater. They stood unscathed, by comparison illustrating the scale of the devastation, testament to the lottery of life. The game of chance that Russian missile strikes inflict on Ukraine. The scene was literally sobering. I donned dark glasses and gave up fighting the wobbly lip. Those photos of the victims peacefully describing every private tragedy. Miles from the frontline, Russia was murdering innocent civilians.

Minutes later we were outside in Anatoliy's favourite restaurant, the mayhem but a block away. You only needed to lean back on your chair to view an incomprehensible level of destruction. Just lean forward again to refocus on the menu and order a tasty salad or lovely shashlik.

More friends arrived. Some I had met before in April. One very jolly chap sat opposite me. Anatoliy very quietly told me that he had been head of the SBU (Ukrainian Security Services) for the Oblast.

"KGB, KGB!" joked Anatoliy, nudging me and carefully teasing his sober friend.

More drink arrived. More shots were poured. More toasts were drunk. Fatally for me, before the food arrived. Remember that rule? I completely forgot about it.

I vaguely remember Krystian and Igor leaving. Kristian looked at me. The look was a pleading, you know this is not going to end well. The sort of stare my wife has given me on similar occasions, with similar disastrous results.

Already our table was a roaring cacophony of testosterone-fuelled anecdotes, speeches and more toasts. The language barrier had by now been comprehensively hurdled. Anatoliy and I swapped stories in a dialect yet to be defined. We hugged each other, laughing in a manner that would frighten any sober person within a 100-metre radius of our table.

I do remember staggering to my feet. My balance issues drawing gasps worthy of any tight rope walker. Anatoliy pushed me in the direction of the gents. My last conscious thoughts were of admiration. The quality of the restaurant's window boxes, outstanding. Beautiful flowers. A fuzzy dream of a warm evening then claimed me. The blur between reality and anxious faces merged into sounds of laughter and a slamming car door.

My next conscious thought was – this is not my blanket? Where was this room? Wait – the floor pattern was the same as our accommodation. I remembered that much. In an instant I was up on my feet. The dehydrated head rush sent me crashing into what was thankfully a door and out into a familiar corridor. I made it to the equally familiar bathroom just in time. Force feeding myself a litre of water I staggered back to bed. Too sick to even begin the detective work of piecing together how I found my way home.

About an hour later, I woke again feeling marginally better. I staggered back into the now day-lit corridor and down to the canteen. Krystian was sat quietly at a table, finishing his breakfast and reading an article on his phone. My appearance in the doorway compelled him to stop what he was doing and look up. I imagined the expression on his face not dissimilar to the one Dr Jekyll would receive from friends after one of his episodes. Like Dr Jekyll I also had no concept or ownership of the monster that had been unleashed.

Krystian tilted his head and regarded me with a curious mix of humour, shock and pity. He took a deep breath and said, "I think you like to know how it happened?"

"How?" I said with the growing fear that I had indeed morphed into a monster.

Krystian roared with laughter as he privately remembered what I could not remember. He tried to speak but burst into more laughter, shaking his head and looking me up and down.

The story that emerged was already marinating in legend and rumour. Apparently, once my disappearance was confirmed, after my failure to return to the table, the team became genuinely concerned. The official curfew was about to begin. It was decided that I must be found. The former head of the local SBU and his comrades, in a scene that must have been part le Carré and part Dad's Army, set out to find me. I suspect it was not the most taxing mission of their careers.

"Have you seen a very drunk Englishman?" was, I believe, the extent of their enquiries. The restaurant staff were able to direct them to my good self, wandering around a car park with the dexterity of a wounded elephant. They had observed me brushing against cars and bouncing off lamp posts, a confused and trapped animal, trying to find its way back to the table. No hope of escape. According to witnesses, getting me into the rescue car had been difficult. But not as difficult as getting me out of the car. By now I was effectively a comatose and occasionally giggling 100 kg lump.

At this point in the story Krystian had to pause again in order to clear himself of another bout of hysterical laughter. Gaining control of himself he kindly continued to describe the challenges of dragging "the lump" to the nearest bed where an old blanket was found to cover the sedated monster. The final indignity came about half an hour later when I was caught drinking and dialling. I had used a secure phone to call my wife to let her know I was OK. The sounds I made on the phone were, according to my wife, unintelligible, frightening and only served to cause distress. Poor Jula. This was perhaps the most unforgivable act of the evening or should I say, early morning.

Igor arrived back fresh and energised by a morning errand. He cast me a look which suggested that in the great "snakes and ladders" game of respect, I had most definitely stepped on a snake.

I looked pleadingly at Kristian whose look signalled, "Give him half an hour."

It was clear that my reputation was in the toilet – along with most of last night's meal. The kindly Krystian ceased being the raconteur and adopted a new role of nurse. A strong coffee was placed in front of me along with a more challenging plate of scrambled eggs. Whilst I struggled with delicate nibbles of egg and toast, Igor looked up from his planning.

"You know you could have died, drinking that much, you know that?"

"He never drinks that much, I can tell, he was out of his league," said my new advocate, Krystian.

I simply nodded and apologised. There was a moment of silence followed by a redemptive peal of laughter.

"He phoned Jula, can you imagine what she's thinking now?" yelled Krystian.

This instigated another round of five-minute belly laughing that even I ended up joining in with. The only

breaks in the mirth filled with Krystian and Igor role playing
Jula's anger, re-calibrating my stupidity with each telling.
Once everyone had calmed down the verdict was clear. My
punishment would come in the form of having to explain my
actions to Jula.

"Where is Anatoliy?" I asked, suddenly aware that he was
nowhere to be seen.

"Hospital," replied Igor looking at his phone.

The word came as a sobering shock.

"I will never do that again Igor. Poor Tolek (short for
Anatoliy), he was having such a good time with his friends."

"Not drinking problem, annual check-up!" replied Igor.
"Tolek not soft like you!"

On cue, Anatoliy came bounding through the door, ready
to roll, beaming at me as if to say, "At least you tried."

DAY 7

HEADING NORTH, MY comrades took pity on me and
let me sit in the back seat of one of the trucks. For reasons
unknown the hangover wore off remarkably quickly. I
consumed three litres of water on the morning leg of the trip
alone! The heat of the day was extraordinary. We stopped for
lunch. Whilst others feasted, I opted for a tentative dry demi-
baguette, each mouthful slowly returning me to human form.

We drove all day. Kristian's eclectic music tastes burning up
the endless highway with sing-songs and stories. By evening we
were heading into our final destination to meet with Ira, one of
our main contacts. Ira has been instrumental in organising and
liaising with multiple parties across the world raising funds and
donations for Ukraine. She, along with two others, Tapac and
Mykola, are extraordinary Ukrainian patriots. We could not do
what we do without their help and support.

JULY CONVOY

Sitting on the beautiful veranda of a café, it was hard to process all that had happened in the space of a week. Looking around us it was just possible to imagine, maybe for a moment, that there was no war - until a group of wounded soldiers limped past or a party of NGO rescue workers asked if they could borrow one of our chairs. Two very burly and bearded English lads were chatting at a table across the way. They nodded at us in solidarity. Everyone was in the same boat. It all felt very Green Park, London 1944. The free world united against tyranny once again.

After a fine feed and me very firmly declining Anatoliy's offer of more drink, Ira and our wonderful hosts took us for an ice cream. In the distance were more smashed buildings. The damage was extensive. The tell-tale signs of a missile attack. The same crushing removal of life and livelihood that we had seen all over Ukraine in the past week. If one were to superimpose all those sites of destruction across Ukraine onto a map of Western Europe, it would approximate the simultaneous destruction of large parts of Madrid, Paris, Frankfurt, Brussels and London. That is the geographical scale of this war.

Cranes and other heavy lifting gear were already in operation. Emergency services were spilling out onto the road. In a panic I finished my ice cream. Wandering past the site of so much suffering with a cornet of chocolate and vanilla would be very poor diplomacy.

Igor was chatting with the security services and soldiers who were helping at the scene. Before I knew it, the cordon tape was being lifted and we were being escorted to the epicentre of the blast. There was that smell again, dustier this time but it was there. Ira was already comforting a lady who was piling some surviving belongings into a wooden crate. Her elderly parents had died in the explosion. The lady was perhaps my age. Hunched, numbed and stooped, her energy had been sapped through hours of weeping.

There was a terrible sense of what now? Where do I go? The authorities were being very kind, yet the sheer catatonic loneliness of that woman will stay with me for a long time. I must be very honest and say that I did not have the courage to comfort her. If I lie to myself, I say it is because I did not speak the language. The truth is that if I had hugged that woman I would have crumbled.

As a merciful distraction some of the soldiers came up to me and asked if I wanted to see their Bakhmut footage. Much easier to watch lads waving, throwing grenades and shooting silhouetted baddies until they no longer move. At the time I reckoned that after the hell of Bakhmut, dealing with rocket damage in a beautiful, sophisticated modern city was an infinitely better posting for those boys. Now looking back, I am not so sure. Being with the lads, being able to hit back directly at the enemy versus witnessing the sudden supersonic oblivion of defenceless civilians? I know which I would choose.

One week to the day after sitting down to lunch with Tania in that shattered little southern Ukrainian town, I was back in Poland by dear Babcia's gravestone with a huge bunch of flowers. We were celebrating her birthday and the good life that she had lived. Babcia's grave sits on a quiet hillside, facing the sea. It is the most beautiful, shaded place which we lovingly tend and visit regularly. She rests where her people know where to find her in remembrance and love. Watching my wife arranging cards and flowers, my mind flashed back to the remains of that decaying Russian soldier, forgotten and in an unknown place. His family will probably never know what happened to him. He too is where he deserves to be. His fate will be the fate of Russia. A decaying, forgotten and unknown place.

JULY CONVOY

GLOSSARY

AC – Air Conditioning

APC – Armoured Personnel Carrier

Bergen - Military Rucksack

Bivvy bag - Waterproof outer covering for a sleeping bag.

Casevac - Casualty Evacuation

CFT – Combat Fitness Test (an annual test carried out by the British Army to assess a soldier's combat readiness)

Day sack - smaller ruck sack

DS – Directing Staff (Training Staff)

FFD - First Field Dressing

FOB - Forward Operating Base

Gortex - Brand of waterproof material

Helly Hansen – popular brand of thermal undervest

Javelin - Anti-tank portable missile system

KGB - Komitet Gosudarstvennoy Bezopasnosti - Former USSR secret services.

MERT - Medical Emergency Response Team

MSR - Main Supply Route

NAAFI - Navy Army and Air Force Institutes

NGO - Non-Governmental Organisation

NLAWS – Next generation Light Anti-tank Weapon

Oblast - Ukrainian word for Region

PASGT Mark - Personnel Armour System for Ground Troops Mark (Helmet)

PTI - Physical Training Instructor

PMC Mercenary - Private Military Contractor

Screech – Powered energy drinks found in UK ration packs. The tart flavour often generates an involuntary screech from the drinker.

UA minders – Ukrainian Army minders. Soldiers who guide aid workers through the military zones.

UXO - Unexploded Ordnance

HOW TOU CAN HELP UKRAINE

THE CONVOYS TO UKRAINE MUST CONTINUE.

If you wish to support the Igor Tracz Foundation,
keeping our vehicles fuelled and, on the road, please donate
what you can. Bank details are given below.

FOUNDATION BANK DETAILS ARE HERE:

IBAN: PL 13160014621745444250000003
kod bic/SWIFT to: PPABPLPK
BNP Paribas Bank Polska S.A.
UL. Kasprzaka 2,
01-211 Warszawa

Or through PayPal please donate to
igorbikejoring@gmail.com

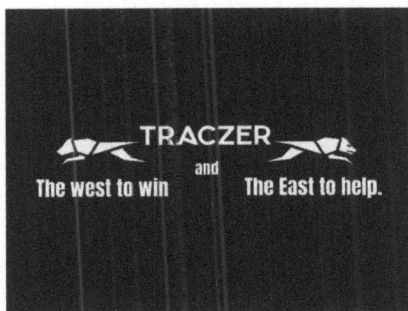

Milton Keynes UK
Ingram Content Group UK Ltd.
UKHW040813060324
438997UK00004B/180